Persistent Images

T0322821

Persistent Images

Encountering Film History in Contemporary Cinema

Andrew Utterson

EDINBURGH
University Press

Edinburgh University Press is one of the leading university presses in
the UK. We publish academic books and journals in our selected subject
areas across the humanities and social sciences, combining cutting-edge
scholarship with high editorial and production values to produce academic
works of lasting importance. For more information visit our website:
edinburghuniversitypress.com

Edinburgh University Press Ltd
The Tun – Holyrood Road
12(2f) Jackson's Entry
Edinburgh EH8 8PJ

First published in hardback by Edinburgh University Press 2020

Typeset in 11/13 Monotype Ehrhardt by
IDSUK (DataConnection) Ltd, and
printed and bound by CPI Group (UK) Ltd,
Croydon, CR0 4YY

A CIP record for this book is available from the British Library

ISBN 978 1 4744 4072 1 (hardback)
ISBN 978 1 4744 4073 8 (paperback)
ISBN 978 1 4744 4074 5 (webready PDF)
ISBN 978 1 4744 4075 2 (epub)

Contents

Figures

Acknowledgements

Any book on cinema would be nigh on impossible without the unwavering support of those with whom one sits in the dark for hour after hour after hour . . . This volume is no different.

Family and friends provided much-needed company during many such hours. More generally, they offered encouragement to write, and the generosity and patience to support this act in all of its many days of cloistered drafting. A special thanks to Frances, including for her help in preparing images.

At Ithaca College, colleagues provided intellectual vitality in their discourses, dialogues and debates. In the area of Screen Studies, inspiration resides in the form of Thomas W. Bohn, Stephen Tropiano and Patricia R. Zimmermann, as well as recent visiting scholars Matthew Holtmeier, Sueyoung Park-Primiano and Chelsea Wessels, and the team of the Finger Lakes Environmental Film Festival. Joshua Bonnetta, alongside others in the area of Cinema and Photography, provided a sounding board for ideas and a wider context of creative practice. The extended community of the Roy H. Park School of Communications housed countless lively discussions and a sense of camaraderie. Wade Pickren and the Center for Faculty Excellence did much to model and develop the value of writing.

In terms of institutional support, the research represented in this book was very generously supported by a sabbatical award through the Office of the Provost and Senior Vice President for Academic Affairs, Ithaca College. Additionally, this book is made possible in part by a James B. Pendleton Grant from the Roy H. Park School of Communications, Ithaca College.

At Cornell University, the role of Regional Visiting Fellow at the Cornell Institute for European Studies (CIES), in the Mario Einaudi Center for International Studies, afforded valuable opportunities for research, while Mary Fessenden and Cornell Cinema provided a vital venue to see and discuss new and old films alike.

At earlier stages of drafting, a whole host of editors, readers, chairs, panellists, respondents, audiences and others contributed enormously to the development of this writing, always willing to prompt and provoke, suggest and steer – in manifold ways, in a multitude of venues. Jane Banks, in turn, offered an expert eye on the path from prose to print.

An earlier version of the first part of Chapter 3 was published as 'On the Movie Theater as Haunted Space: Spectral Spectatorship and Existential Historiography in Abbas Kiarostami's *Shirin*' in *Quarterly Review of Film and Video*, 33.8 (2016): 685–706, and is reprinted by kind permission of Taylor & Francis (doi.org/10.1080/10509208.2016.1144030).

An earlier version of Chapter 4 was published as 'Water Buffalo, Catfish, and Monkey Ghosts: The Transmigratory Materialities of *Uncle Boonmee Who Can Recall His Past Lives*' in *New Review of Film and Television Studies*, 15.2 (2017): 231–49, and is reprinted by kind permission of Taylor & Francis (doi.org/10.1080/17400309.2017.1311088).

An earlier version of Chapter 5 was published as 'Goodbye to Cinema? Jean-Luc Godard's *Adieu au langage* as 3D Images at the Edge of History' in *Studies in French Cinema*, 19.1 (2019): 69–84, and is reprinted by kind permission of Taylor & Francis (doi.org/10.1080/14715880.2016.1242045).

Last, I would be remiss if I did not also recognise and thank the editors and team at Edinburgh University Press, all of whom provided their own invaluable support of this book, from conception to completion. Gillian Leslie, as commissioning editor, offered the spur of initial interest, while Richard Strachan, in his own editorial role, has been steadfast in his support as the project has taken shape.

Without all of these countless contributions, the book-bound realisation of my own particular encounters with film history would simply not have occurred.

Introduction

In the wake of the oft-presumed demise and obsolescence of cinema, its past continues to find presence in the present. Yet, if the memory of cinema persists, it does so in technologically and otherwise reconfigured forms, requiring increasingly creative conceptions of history and time. For the historian attuned to these altered states, contemporary cinema tells its own history (or histories). After all, as this book illustrates in its specific case studies, cinema – including its cumulative archive of images – has demonstrated a remarkable resilience, an unwillingness to be buried or forgotten, resonating in the present in the most surprising and illuminating of ways.

Looking simultaneously backwards and forwards, in these filmic works and their textual analyses, this book argues for the necessity of reflective as well as reflexive ways of thinking about history, in which the interactions of past and present offer up an ongoing space of creative and historical renewal. Where contemporary cinema grasps the capacity to look back, to dig below the surface of film history in its own acts of media archaeology, the traces of the past find revised meaning.

To document cinema at the exact points of encounter between texts and technologies, history and historiography, as *Persistent Images: Encountering Film History in Contemporary Cinema* seeks to do, is to engage a series of (self-)inscriptions of time and memory that can themselves offer methods and means, models and metaphors for reimagining cinema and reframing its history. Cinema persists in an array of encounters that carry this history into the present, through processes and practices of transformative remembrance.

CINEMATIC–MNEMONIC ENCOUNTERS

The cinematic–mnemonic encounter, that is, the meeting of mediation and memory, beckons the historian. It is a means of mapping the memory of cinema in the interstices of the physical archive of film history and the mnemonic archive of cultural memory, as negotiated in contemporary cinematic texts. At this site of encounter, film history is variously translated and transmuted across temporal registers and spatial dimensions.

In these encounters, the intersections of past and present are zones of connection. To encounter film history in contemporary cinema, as do each of the works that this book considers, is to place past and present in dynamic dialogue. The encounters elaborated are multi-directional, in which the memory of cinema is actively sought, and in which history ruptures and revisits the present in unexpected and unpredictable ways.

This book outlines a series of such encounters with film history as represented in contemporary cinema and the curatorial framing of the cinematic experience. These are works that approach head-on the historical legacy and memory of cinema as one means of advancing our knowledge of the medium. Most explicitly, the encounters in question are with contemporary films that reveal the past as now aesthetically mediated, technologically inscribed, reflexively explored and historiographically framed.

Indeed, these are encounters with sounds and images that take on new valences of meaning in the present, in terms of revised forms of history and signification and the ontological implications of this presence (or absence) in the present. All of these must be encountered and theorised anew.

To encounter film history in the present is also to witness a history that is marked in relief in important ways. These include images and experiences that occupy the slippages between material and immaterial markers of time. Film history, for example, exists also in the shape of ghosts, spectres and other hauntings of a history that refuses to be consigned to the past and whose resonances have become essential to our understanding of the medium.

Crucially, the encounter also exists as a site of transformative potential. In the exchange of contemporary cinema and historical memory, we find the possibility of mutual transformation of past and present. This encounter can shine new light on the cinematic corpus in one historical trajectory or direction, while engaging this past as a route towards sustaining the vitality of cinema in the other by way of cinematic works that return to the history of the medium as the means to rethink it in the present (and, by implication, the future).

Spanning approximately a decade of such encounters (the contemporary cinema of the title), this book details a series of films and related texts, projects and discourses that take as their explicit subject film history. Specifically, this is an international selection of films and filmmakers that deal with this history in self-conscious ways. The selection is deliberately eclectic, across geography (Russia, Thailand, France, Iran and further) and authorship (representing a range of different directors) as well as modes (narrative, documentary and other).

What each of these works has in common is their conscious relationship with the past. On the levels of form and content, they implicitly and explicitly engage film history to uncover new understandings of past and present, which this book strives to document and to which it aims to contribute. At the essence of these understandings are the fundamental concerns of artistic reinvention and historical revelation, at once cognisant of a historical moment (questions about the continued existence of the medium, for example), while also exploring the ways by which we might view the evolution of media across time. In these acts of historical reflection, film history is rewritten in real time (or, at least, cinematic time) as the moving image becomes one means of recounting its own past.

With this concern with history at the fore, irrespective of geography, whether in narrative or documentary forms, these films coalesce around the realm of global art cinema. This milieu lends itself to a certain consciously cinematic or cinephilic culture and offers the opportunity to foreground and explore what might be anathema to more commercially oriented or popular cinemas, even if the technological and other changes represented in these films are not exclusive to them.

Indeed, in terms of scope and methodology across the course of these encounters, the intention is not to suggest a fixed and finite body of work, nor a tendency that defines all or even most of contemporary cinema. Rather, the aim is to look at a number of notable works in greater detail as a way to highlight certain facets of film history that are manifested in these thematic and aesthetic representations. This book also illustrates a method – a particular application of textual analysis focusing on the workings of form and style that aims to contribute to ways of thinking that are more typically the preserve of historiography. Put another way, this selection of films is not designed to offer an exhaustive survey of the countless ways in which contemporary cinema might depict or otherwise comment on the history of the medium, but rather to elucidate specific examples of how it might do so, explicating and contextualising vis-à-vis relevant historical frameworks and theoretical debates. For this reason, this book generally combines the approaches of media archaeology and concepts of historiographic application with the specificity of film history and the closer focus on the textual analysis of individual films.

Additionally, if these encounters are with sound and image, they are also encounters with and through a changing technological apparatus – a notion adopted in relatively broad terms to refer to a set of technologies and tools, materials and architectures, which have historically constituted the means for the production and dissemination of the moving image and the cinematic experience. Technology both maps and marks film history, embodying and communicating it in the present. History is also told in this apparatus, its aesthetic applications as well as the meanings it assumes over time. The lenses and frames of the moving image, for example, offer fruitful means of revisioning the past. As such, each chapter and its case study or studies contemplates the nature and status of contemporary cinema by way of inventive takes on its apparatus as a path to the historical. This book is organised to address a range of areas of technological change, exploring a variety of imaging technologies, the materials (or immateriality) of the medium, and the sites and technologies of exhibition, among other aspects of a broader cinematic apparatus. Contemporary tools and technologies rub shoulders with film history – extended and emergent – in a series of authorial visions that channel the history of a medium through its evolution.

As an initial encounter, in Chapter 1 this book begins its quest for the memory of cinema with a symbolic act of media archaeology as historical discovery. It pursues the buried pasts and the material as well as immaterial legacies of film history, sensitive to the traces of a medium, whether precisely defined (in terms of the materiality of celluloid or photochemical film) or more generally defined (as an art form whose historical transformations are also the subject of the remainder of this book). This chapter engages the past through a burrowing down – literally as well as figuratively – in a (media) archaeological dig into the residue of the past. In the discussion of Bill Morrison's *Dawson City: Frozen Time* (2016), there is a larger effort to unearth and uncover film history and provide a description of its resonant return.

Offering another apparatus-specific angle as a contemporary vantage point to the archives of cultural memory and cinematic images, Chapter 2 likewise takes its cue from media archaeological models. This time, however, it looks upwards rather than downwards in search of film history in material and immaterial objects and phenomena. This history is here embodied not in reels of film, as in the previous chapter, but in imaging devices themselves. The camera-carrying drone is the principal focus for this historical inquiry, analysing Aleksandr Sokurov's *Francofonia* (2015), a film that likewise imbricates historical memory and cinematic memory, in this instance through the multiple histories of aerial photography and its recent cinematic iterations or incarnations. To look towards the skies, this chapter suggests, is to encounter history, time and memory, manifest not only in the forms and functions of technologies but in their aesthetic expressions, too.

Returning us to the earth and a further cinematic journey of topography and time, Chapter 3 focuses on the shifting significations associated with the movie theatre as a symbol of architecture and apparatus, the cinematic experience and its trace. Abbas Kiarostami's *Shirin* (2008), and its meta-cinematic representation of the movie theatre, is considered in mapped dialogue with a broadly contemporaneous curatorial project that documents the psychogeographies and mnemonic resonances of moviegoing, past and present. Comparisons are drawn between the anonymous patrons of Kiarostami's movie theatre in *Shirin* as reflexive phantasm and the relocation of a site-specific phenomenology to the streets of London, as documented in Iain Sinclair's *70x70: Unlicensed Preaching: A Life Unpacked in 70 Films* (2014), a cine-biography and related project of site-specific screenings. The focus is on charting cinematic cartographies as spatialised media archaeology that brings memory and experience into historical and historiographic focus.

Turning from the movie theatre to the underlying medium of the films historically screened in such spaces, the encounter in Chapter 4 is one of transmigratory materialities, and a look back at the film-to-digital transition of recent years as textually refracted in historiographic analogy. Specifically, this chapter investigates the intertwined technological, ontological and historical status of a filmic base, i.e. photochemical film, precisely as it came to exist as a principally historical medium. Ideas of corporeal finitude and material obsolescence are explored through Apichatpong Weerasethakul's *Uncle Boonmee Who Can Recall His Past Lives* (*Loong Boonmee raleuk chat*, 2010), in terms of its representations of transmigration and reincarnation, with a particular focus on its use of Super 16mm film at a time in cinema history when photochemical film of all kinds was experiencing its own existential transformation. This formal strategy serves as the starting point for an exploration of a cinematic life cycle that includes, but also exceeds, the historiographic conceptions or tropes of birth and death.

Moving from the materials of cinematic encounter to the dimensions in which they are encountered, Chapter 5 regards film history with the distinct ocular perspective of 3D cinema. Its principal case studies are Jean-Luc Godard's 3D feature film *Goodbye to Language* (*Adieu au langage*, 2014) and its preceding 3D short *The Three Disasters* (*Les trois désastres*, 2013), in which the history of an entire medium is evoked using the apparatus of contemporary 3D imaging. Intertextual vectors of love and death are charted in the so-called *z*-dimension of 3D stereoscopy, with a cinephilia concerned with archival images and an interest in rebooting this history as literally and metaphorically reframed. The now-3D cinematic image projects its own history, including its technologies and a broader historiography that concerns the prospective passing – or *adieu* – of cinema.

To conclude, and serving as an afterword of sorts, Chapter 6 further considers the spatialised contours of film history, now in the altered dimensions of large-format screens (namely IMAX) and macro-historical schemes. This chapter contemplates an entire universe of light and shadow and the parallel histories and geneses of cosmic time and cinematic time. Reflecting the opening chapter, which situates the stratified layers of earthly deposits as both a physical repository and historiographic metaphor for the stores of cinematic memory, this closing chapter expands to the history of the universe, examining Terrence Malick's IMAX documentary *Voyage of Time: The IMAX Experience* (2016). The IMAX screen on which this experience is exhibited offers a formal and aesthetic corollary between a physically expanded work (in terms of the 70mm film frame and IMAX projection) and the larger historical framework of the birth and death of the cosmos. *Voyage of Time* visualises the expanses of the universe, most obviously, but also the cosmos or constellation of cinema's own technologies, screens and images. In this sense, the journey through the history of the universe that constitutes the film's titular voyage might also be usefully read as a voyage of visuality, an expanded history of the moving image itself.

By way of these historical – and historiographic – encounters, this book endeavours to detail a cinema whose past remains palpable in the present. If it begins by zooming in, digging into the earth and the past in the stratified layers of film history, it ends by zooming out, placing the multiple screens and images of cinema within a deep temporal framework of millions of years and the infinite path of light and shadow. Along the way, in its span of encounters, this book identifies the persistent images of a cinema whose memory is encountered in many forms, as represented in and via its evolving apparatus.

Collectively, these encounters offer new ways of thinking about film history and contemporary cinema alike. Ultimately, with the aim of channelling the memory of cinema into the future, the emphasis is on this retrospective engagement with film history as a means of reimagining it in the technological and aesthetic transformations of a range of experimental practices. Contemporary cinema, it is argued, reflects on this history as a means to reconceptualise the medium. At the very edge of this history, it is the continued resonance of the past – in all the variations encountered in this book – that is at the core of a reflexively aware contemporary cinema and a progressive historiography that might account for it.

CHAPTER I

Media Archaeology and the Memory of a Medium: *Dawson City: Frozen Time*

What does it mean to encounter the memory of cinema long after its residue has been consigned to the past, abandoned or forgotten in the simultaneous decay of memory and matter? What, in particular, might be revealed by those who take on the archaeological task of uncovering layers of cinematic sediment?

Situating the contemporary moment as one where we might negotiate the cumulative archive of cinema and our cultural memory of the moving image, this chapter begins its historical task with one such analysis. It is a geological as well as an archaeological endeavour. Specifically, the emphasis is on the legacy of film and the cinematic layering of memory as filmic substrate, in a combination of erosion and eruption, accretion and avulsion, deposition and uplift.

To extend our historical approach, we might consider the directionality and flows of images across time. As well as digging down through layers of film history and their corresponding ages in the act of historical inquiry, there is also the possibility of the persistence of the past, when that which is buried or forgotten emerges, rising up through the matter of time. The moving image is not only sought in an exploratory excavation, but, as this chapter will demonstrate, it might also return unbidden from the past and rise to the surface of the present.

As an illustrative case study, Bill Morrison's *Dawson City: Frozen Time* (2016) represents one such encounter. It is a film explicitly concerned with archaeologies and geologies as historical concepts and historiographic strategies, using them in particular to engage cinematic histories. Media archaeology is rendered literal, illustrating the material and immaterial traces of a film history that reveals both the elemental geology of earthly deposits – its own photochemical past – and the temporal transformations of this filmic matter. It engages not just the materiality of a medium but the mnemonic resonance of this history, as aesthetically articulated and further mediated.

DAWSON CITY: *FROZEN TIME*: FILM HISTORY FROM BELOW

As the history of cinema is unearthed in *Dawson City: Frozen Time*, the deep time of cinema becomes also frozen time, and vice versa. The ground beneath us – *terra firma* – also becomes *tempora firma* – with the temporal dimension of history now registered through the geological sediment of archaeological discovery.

This principally found-footage documentary focuses on the cinematic history of Dawson City, a gold rush settlement in the Yukon Territory, north-west Canada, which grew rapidly with the discovery of gold and its prospecting in the 1890s. What had hitherto been a sparsely populated area was radically changed by the gold strike. The film details the burial and subsequent exhumation of a veritable treasure trove of cinema, deposited in the ground as refuse amid the clamour for precious elements, only to be fortuitously preserved by the particular climatic conditions of the Canadian permafrost. This site would reveal its own deposits – not of gold, but of the silver screen – decades later when they were disturbed and uncovered in the 1970s. Via a range of archival as well as contemporary sources, including silent films of various kinds (with a particular emphasis on those found in Dawson City), the unique story of the Yukon gold rush is interwoven with a wider cinematic history.

Coincidentally or otherwise, the growth of Dawson City and the transformation of its discarded films into cinematic gold echoes the riches of cinema in general as a mass medium, reflecting its own development in what is typically referred to as the birth or invention of this medium, both as an art form and its material base of photochemical film.

The material history of *Dawson City: Frozen Time* intersects a broader interest – in the film and this chapter – in the continuing resonance of history more generally. The particular context of the Yukon gold rush constitutes microcosmic and metaphorical consideration of cinema and how we might archivally preserve but also creatively reimagine its past.

In the midst of Dawson City's rush for gold, what is the value of cinema, both in terms of its underlying materials and the cultural memory conveyed via this material base as its own precious element? What special properties did cinema once hold, and might we still bring them to light by way of its trace elements – whether solely metaphorical or also literal, as in the case of Dawson City – and the temporal sediment of film history, more universally?

Unearthing Cinema

In *Dawson City: Frozen Time*, in a process of digging – through earth and time – the deposits of the past offer up a site of cinematic memory. In terms of historiography, conceptions of media archaeology and geology interweave in a number of ways, suggesting multiple routes towards the return of film history beyond the particular geographical and historical extremities of the frozen north and the specific circumstances of Dawson City's accidental archive. The Yukon soil reveals film history, including its material base, as archived across time and now recontextualised and represented in the present, as the fields of archaeology and geology offer means for mining this past.

Indeed, in terms of how we might approach film history more generally, archaeology – digging down, in one way or another, in one site or another – offers multiple ways of thinking about this history and the act of historiography. In the instance of *Dawson City: Frozen Time*, a geological history is especially apt in terms of the relationship between cinema as a physical medium and a parallel definition of the term of cinema as mass cultural form.

Invoking precisely the practices of archaeology – and, by implication, media archaeology – Morrison himself describes *Dawson City: Frozen Time* as 'a sort of archaeological dig' (Crafton with Morrison 2018: 96), adding further that '[i]t is a history, or historiography, of the image' (Crafton with Morrison 2018: 98). Put simply, if this is an archaeological film in the most straightforward sense of the term, discovered by sifting through the soil for artefacts of the past, it is also a metaphor for historiographic exploration and historical discovery.

Media archaeology, as a field of historiography and related theory, foregrounds the explicit aim of charting new genealogies of media histories, mapping unexpected trajectories in order to complicate established teleologies. For Thomas Elsaesser, discussing film history as media archaeology, the emphasis is on 'parallel histories' and 'alternative trajectories' (Elsaesser 2016: 25), with the ultimate intention of 'not just the excavation of manifold pasts but also generating an archaeology of possible futures' (Elsaesser 2016: 25).

Meanwhile, the particular branch or subset of geological thinking, outlined most explicitly in Jussi Parikka's *A Geology of Media* (Parikka 2015), opens up further ways of approaching such media, including cinema. In the application of geology as a media archaeological concept, the physical elements of film – nitrocellulose, camphor and so on – would be laid bare in a media ecosystem, placing the industrial extraction, exploitation and disposal of film within elemental taxonomies (as a form of geology) and expanded temporalities (as a form of archaeology).

Notably, such archaeological-geological discovery is not always by way of a search downwards, a burrowing into the ground, but can also encompass an unanticipated return to the surface. In geological terms, in considering the temporal spans of what he describes as the *Deep Time of the Media* (2006 [2002]), Siegfried Zielinski opens up such ideas of history, including in reference to 'a dynamic cycle of erosion, deposition, consolidation, and uplifting before erosion starts the cycle anew' (Zielinski 2006 [2002]: 4). Of particular relevance to

Dawson City: Frozen Time are those cycles associated with patterns of deposition and uplift – even if, in the instance of Dawson City, such natural cycles are also subject to the decidedly unnatural forces of human intervention.

For Parikka, though his practice of media archaeology is sometimes in tension with Zielinski's, they are linked to the idea of cosmological genesis, including reconfigured historical and temporal scales by way of fossilised pasts and the evolutionary weave of time. Parikka links the geological and the temporal by arguing that geology simultaneously uncovers the past and the future. As he puts it, '[d]epth becomes time' (Parikka 2015: 13). If the explicit span of *Dawson City: Frozen Time* does not extend to the scientific scales of deep time in the strictest terms (of millions of years, for example), the titular reference to frozen time nevertheless situates us firmly within an earthly realm of temporal suspension and/or expansion.

In these interlinked notions of archaeology and geology, conceptions that often overlap in *Dawson City: Frozen Time*, the depths of the earth would both conceal and reveal a cinematic archive, its own store of arrested time in the form of moving images, emerging into the present only through successive acts of archaeological as well as media archaeological discovery.

Celluloid Sediment

In this story of celluloid sediment, from nitrate to substrate, and the industrial exploitation of film in a city better known for its mining of gold, Dawson City would become, too, a cinematic city, and a proxy for a wider film history and the material base that carries its images.

As Morrison's film depicts it, during Dawson City's rapid growth, the emergence of cinema would play an important role, in many respects typical of the public's burgeoning appetite for this new medium. By the 1910s, multiple venues screened films to a city whose population now numbered in the thousands. As the furthermost point of a national distribution circuit, Dawson City functioned as an industrial terminus. After films were screened, most of the prints, their exhibition function having been served, would be stored or discarded rather than returned to the source. As the onscreen text explains:

> Films could take two or three years to arrive in Dawson after they were originally released. Distributors were unwilling to pay for the return carriage of the out-of-date films once they had screened in Dawson. And so many films were disposed of in the traditional manner [i.e. dumped into the Yukon River].

As well as being cast into the waters of the Yukon, other stores of film were destroyed as a combustible spectacle, set alight in public bonfires. The films, having served a particular use value, were now discarded into the environment with abandon.

Fascinating though it is, Dawson City and its own mining of cinematic matter suggests a bigger history, the parallel gold rush of the rise of cinema as a modern medium. For Scott MacDonald, these intersecting histories (the gold rush of the Yukon and the emergence of cinema) can be considered more precisely in terms of the particular materialities of cinema, namely the medium of photochemical film. He contends that 'Morrison's excavation of the sudden rise and gradual fall of Dawson can be read as a metaphor for the history of celluloid cinema itself' (MacDonald 2016: 40), arguing the interconnectedness of the gold rush and film as its own form of commodity. The particular trajectory of a newly founded city rooted in the spectacular appeal of commodifiable pleasures serves as a parallel to cinema, no matter the less precious elements that comprise the chemicals and other constituents of film.

Indeed, the material base of cinema comes to the fore in *Dawson City: Frozen Time*. Alongside gold, key elements include those materials on which moving images were photographed and printed, as films were distributed and exhibited in cities around the globe including Dawson City. To provide some perspective, Morrison outlines the extended lineage of these materials. Onscreen text notes that '[c]ellulose nitrate was discovered in 1846 by combining cotton with nitric and sulphuric acids'. This text is shown over archival footage of the materials in question – in this instance, at the Eastman Kodak Company plant in Rochester,

Figure 1.1 *The Romance of Celluloid* as excerpted in *Dawson City: Frozen Time*

New York as excerpted from a short Metro-Goldwyn-Mayer documentary, *The Romance of Celluloid* (Anon., 1937). In the film, the mined materials of salts and silver are illustrated as ingredients in this industrial recipe. Vats of chemicals depict the mixing of camphor and gun cotton to create the flexible, plasticised photographic rolls that were Eastman Kodak's stock in trade, as coated with a light-sensitive emulsion to create cellulose nitrate or nitrate film – better known as celluloid.

If this is a romance, as the title of the 1937 film implies, it is one born of a decidedly industrial imaginary, oblivious to the environmental implications of its own use of natural resources, or of the archival safekeeping of this photographic base and the images it was intended to capture. Approximately eighty years later, in the context of the predominantly post-filmic present, *The Romance of Celluloid* takes on an extra valence of meaning, situated somewhere between heightened cinephilic yearning and a bittersweet reminder of lost love.

The images of *The Romance of Celluloid* also suggest a recurring meaning in *Dawson City: Frozen Time*, in terms of the volatility of an underlying medium whose lineage is rooted as much in the acts of war as the art of cinema. As an antecedent of photochemical film, we are reminded that the addition of nitric and sulphuric acids to cotton created an explosive (aka gun cotton) that was only later developed into film. Footage of cellulose nitrate in *Dawson City: Frozen Time* illustrates this explosive combination as used in munitions applications long before still photography and moving images.

In an elemental confluence of fire and ice, this emphasis on the celluloid history of Dawson City coincides with the era of cinema in which nitrate film was the standard film format, regardless of its inherent instability. 'Film was born of an explosive', notes the onscreen text, adding its own layer of meaning to the archival footage. In this instance, the images depict a reel of the cellulose nitrate that comprised most of the film stock used in the first decades of cinema. The explosive properties of nitrate would lead to countless fires at factories and facilities, including in Dawson City.

Accordingly, nitrate film offers its own metaphorical potential, as visualised in archival footage of burning reels of this material prone to spontaneous combustion, recalling the decades prior to the introduction of acetate safety stock in the late 1940s and early 1950s. Images of razed theatres, factories, archives and charred reels of film become a recurring symbol.

In this new context, the motif and narrative recounting of fire after fire remind us, among other things, of the impermanence of film – whether nitrate or otherwise – as the physical carrier of images whose ephemeral flicker was the product of the cinematic dream factory. In one instance, *Dawson City: Frozen Time* depicts the explosion at the Solax Film Company (co-founded by filmmaker Alice Guy-Blaché) using archival newsreel of the event from *International News, Vol. 1, Issue 52* (Anon., 1919), one of those films later discarded in Dawson City. Moving from reportage to requiem, this footage is immediately followed by shots from Guy-Blaché's Solax-produced *The Pit and the Pendulum* (1913), also part of the Dawson City archive and thus buried by ice after other Solax films had perished by fire. Now, more than a century later, as smoke is seen billowing from the factory, the photochemical film used to document this blaze is itself distressed by the passage of time, creating organic forms of degradation and decay over which a still image of Guy-Blaché is superimposed.

Elsewhere, we are reminded of the 1914 explosion at Thomas Edison's film manufacturing plant in West Orange, New Jersey, depicted not directly but by way of a later newsreel from *British Canadian Pathé News, 13A* (Anon., 1920), another of the Dawson City films. This footage shows Edison himself working with liquid chemicals in a laboratory, through a haze of water damage to the photochemical film that now offers its own associated metaphor for corrosive decay.

In all of these instances, the materiality of nitrate film points to the more general ephemerality of cinema, and to the medium itself as historically defined by the prospect of obsolescence. From the earliest days of cinema, film contained the elemental properties for its own demise – if not by immolation, then by other forms of disposal or deterioration. By design or otherwise, film is a medium perpetually needing to overcome its destruction.

Dawson City: Frozen Time also points to the impermanence of the architecture in which such films were exhibited – in this instance, the boom and bust of an exhibition infrastructure at the accelerated scale of the rise and fall of a gold rush town. The movie theatre constituted the cultural locus or site of social gathering in a newly developing Dawson City, whose growth largely mirrored, in historical terms, the proliferation of cinema and its own rapid curve of adoption in the 1890s and early twentieth century.

Later, as the population of Dawson City left as quickly as it arrived, these movie theatres would be repurposed or destroyed. The settings within which Dawson City's films were contained also reveal the conditions in which cinema existed – and still exists – as a site of cultural memory, a further archaeological legacy that Stephen Barber has described more generally in terms of an architecture of 'abandoned images' (Barber 2010).

The abandonment that would consign Dawson City's films to the earth was one of burial, the marking of a death or passing in which the surrounding rubble and ruins that would come to contain a cinematic corpse serve as coffin, crypt or tomb. Such a reading is encouraged by the terms of loss and lamentation that describe a larger absence – from Dawson City to every city. 'It is estimated that 75% of all silent films have been lost', explains the onscreen text, with its stark narrational reminder placed over images from a British Pathé documentary, *The Preservation of Cine Film* (Anon., 1967). In this context, this film is perhaps more fittingly titled per its original French,

Images en péril (in direct English translation, *Images in Peril* or *Images at Risk*), given its depiction of nitrate film as ravaged over time. The documentary also connects death and decay as metaphor and analogy, long before Paolo Cherchi Usai would popularise this notion in his groundbreaking work on the archival precarity of film and its postulation of 'the death of cinema' (Cherchi Usai 2001), describing the materiality and mutability of the medium of film and its own decay, decomposition or death.

In Dawson City, with regard to its own imperilled images, preservation would occur only through the serendipity of subterranean storage, when decades' worth of films were lowered into the ground as landfill below new construction in 1929. Clifford T. Thomson retrospectively described (in a 15 August 1978 letter to the *Klondike Korner*, as quoted in *Dawson City: Frozen Time*) the circumstances by which this cinematic cache came to be buried below an ice rink:

> The library was filling up to capacity and we wrote the film people about the fact and they instructed us to destroy hundreds of film[s]. [. . .] It occurred to me they would make excellent fill for the old swimming hole in the ice arena [. . .], we trucked them into the arena and dumped them in the swimming hole. I felt sure that they would never be found and they would integrate into rubbish and dirt as they were well covered with earth.

In this way, cinema would become yet another source of industrial waste in this city of gold. Films were returned to the earth from which their own constituent elements were once mined, for a fleeting filmic incarnation, now disposed of in the most careless of ways – wantonly, both with regard to environmental consequences and equally oblivious to cultural heritage.

Yet, through a process of environmental recycling, the earth would ultimately give up its buried refuse, mined once more, not for the stores of gold that had forged the city's past, but for the cinematic treasures that would soon be uncovered. The films of Dawson City would lie in their cryogenic chamber awaiting discovery, whether by chance or purpose. This would occur nearly half-a-century later in this archaeological tale of elemental return.

If historiographic conceptions of cinema have long since incorporated discourses of mortality as an existential metaphor (see, for example, Bazin 2014 [1953]), in the instance of Dawson City, the corpse (reel after reel of discarded films) would rise to the surface as if resisting its premature burial, and not unlike the cycles of uplift described in the field of geology. As early as 1938, as *Dawson City: Frozen Time* details, the *Dawson Daily News* reported the following, under the headline 'Children Finding Much Movie Film':

As the rink of the Dawson Amateur Hockey League is being repaired many youngors [youngsters] have been attracted to the premises with an unlooked-for result that could end in severe results.

It appears the former swimming tank, in the centre of the rink, had been used in the distant past as a depository for discarded movie film by the D.A.A. Theatre, adjoining, and some of the wee visitors have found strips of the film sticking out of the dirt and, upon further examination, have found they could haul out much of it, to their great delight.

The film is very combustible and when ignited burns swiftly and with great heat, so should any of the youngsters who are playing with it take a notion to set it afire the result could be disastrous. Therefore, the children should be cautioned to leave the film where found.

Four decades later, in 1978, a construction crew happened upon this accidental archive while working on an unrelated project. The reels of film were discovered in the earth, some protected by metal canisters, others simply loose, unspooled and now soiled among the rubble. The unexpected encounter led to a pause in construction to allow the site to be appraised – media archaeology in its most literal of manifestations.

Figure 1.2 Unearthed film as documented in *Dawson City: Frozen Time*

Sam Kula was the Director of the National Film, Television and Sound Archives Division of the National Archives of Canada at the time of the Dawson City find and was brought in to help assess the materials being pulled from the earth:

> My first estimates, based on the film that lay close to the surface, were that we would only be able to salvage a few of the reels and, at that, only a small portion of each reel. The base was in surprisingly good shape after nearly fifty years, but seepage from the spring thaws had bleached most of the image. The emulsion had been attacked by chemicals in the soil and by chemicals released in the decomposition of both the metal reels on which the film was mounted and the metal transfer cases in which the reels were packed (six to eight reels to a box). [. . .]
> The first reports by telephone, a week later, led to a very hasty revision of the estimates. There were a great many more films to be recovered in the roughly twenty-by-thirty-foot hole than we had originally calculated. The films close to the surface were heavily damaged by water, but the films below them were emerging in much better condition, although affected by the damp and corrosion. Many of them had leaders and titles in good enough shape to allow positive identification, and some were even equipped with censor bands and shipping instructions. (Kula 1979: 16–17)

Ironically, the permafrost itself had protected these films from destruction, whether by natural or other causes. Ultimately, numerous works were salvaged in this site of impromptu preservation and newly ascribed archaeological significance. Approximately half-a-million feet of nitrate film was transported to the National Archives, a find that spans the first three decades of the twentieth century, including films from as early as 1903 and as late as 1929. Specifically, the Dawson City material comprises 533 reels of film, including the sole surviving sources of 372 works, by directors including Tod Browning, D. W. Griffith, the aforementioned Guy-Blaché, Maurice Tourneur, Lois Weber and others.

Approximately a year after the initial discovery, and after painstaking cataloguing and restoration on the part of the National Archives and others (including the US Library of Congress), these films would be screened in Dawson City once more, at the Palace Grand Theatre, in 1979. They emerged into an altogether different Dawson City, and into an equally altered cinematic moment, a legacy further complicated by Morrison's mediation.

Excavation as Animation

Over time, the base materials or elements of cinema were transformed – rendered precious, perhaps, but certainly changed at the very least – and images mined from the past take on new life in the present. This is the case with the altered historicity of the Dawson City films, including the significations associated with the material mediations of an elementally shaped physical form. In this sense, the Dawson City film find also constitutes a technological and aesthetic inscription of a wider film history, excavated and animated alike.

In terms of the most tangible markers of degradation, for example, these films find new meanings in historical, cultural and other contexts. If these films have been preserved or frozen in time, in many instances they are also physically marked as a result of this stasis. Throughout *Dawson City: Frozen Time*, the material properties of film are foregrounded in the recovered images, illustrating the conditions that caused the decay that now becomes both a historical canvas and an aesthetic component of the films.

In one such instance, *Dawson City: Frozen Time* describes and illustrates the process of water damage and its resulting patterning over images of these geologically imprinted and temporally rendered visual effects. A montage of excerpts provides an illustration of some of the films that bear these marks of earth and time.[1] If these films represent relatively generic fare in dramatic terms, the degree to which their images have been changed also transforms them into something else entirely, recontextualised as visual vectors of historical signification. What these images now have in common is the visual play of cellular forms. Patination of physical damage is foregrounded rather than effaced, with the original figurative components of each frame distorted by and in dynamic with the encroaching decay.

If an emphasis on the impermanence of film and the visual and other qualities of the materials of cinema is authorially consistent with Morrison's larger body of work,[2] and while *Dawson City: Frozen Time* can clearly be read in terms of the material properties of film per se, there are also aesthetic and historiographic particularities to the Dawson City archive. Notably, the specific conditions of the soil of Dawson City led to a distinctive variation of filmic decay with its own unique visual imprint of time and place, a terroir of site-specific degradation. Water damage, as opposed to other types of nitrate decay, here results in characteristic visual flaring, particularly marked around the edges of the frame. Morrison describes this distinction thus:

> With nitrate decay, the image bends and buckles as the nitrate base slowly transforms over time beneath the emulsion. [. . .]
>
> The Dawson City collection, on the other hand, was fairly well preserved in its frozen tomb, and ironically does not show that much nitrate decay to the base. What you do see with the Dawson collection is considerable water damage, which it largely suffered once it was exhumed from its burial place. This is seen as the white streaks on the margin of the frame – the distinctive 'Dawson flutter', as it is known in archival circles, which seems to sit on top of the image like a flickering patina, but does not appear to alter the shape and form of the image as with the nitrate decay. (Morrison cited in Macaulay 2017)

The water damage of *Dawson City: Frozen Time* inhabits the frame like a phantasm, a reading reinforced by the circumstances of the burial of these films, so long forgotten in their unmarked grave. When the central protagonists of *The Butler and the Maid* are depicted in a scene drawn from the Dawson City archive, the human figure of the maid is almost entirely obliterated by visual decay, with much of the image whited out, as if painted, scratched or otherwise treated. Similarly, in footage from *Polly of the Circus*, an already uncanny scene of a woman staring into the unknown is lent otherworldly quality by the patina that surrounds her as a filmic apparition.

More generally, in terms of how we might account for this footage beyond formal abstraction per se, the Dawson City backdrop further amplifies the links between such decay on the one hand, and metaphorical considerations of materially mediated signifiers of time on the other. If the degradation of these films is decidedly physical in nature, the materiality of film also functions as a metaphor for a broader understanding of film history and the gradual loss or erasure of historical and cultural memory.

At one point, *Dawson City: Frozen Time* excerpts a short British Pathé portrait of the city, *Dawson: Gold Rush Memories* (Anon., 1961). This film, already evocative in the early 1960s of the memorial capacity of cinema, remains apt in its title, with a sense of history remediated or recontextualised still further, in 2016 with the additional decades of time and the scrutiny of memory of *Dawson City: Frozen Time*. Over images of the contemporaneous

Figure 1.3 *Polly of the Circus* as excerpted in *Dawson City: Frozen Time*

Dawson City, voiceover narration in the 1961 film, now represented in 2016, describes how

> Dawson City sprang up overnight. A rip-roaring shack town where the only cheap thing was human life, where a lucky man could pluck a fortune out of the earth. All that went with those days is now only a memory. But what days they were while they lasted.

Layers of cinematic time are accumulated or accreted atop one another in *Dawson City: Frozen Time*, which will come to exist as its own sedimentary matter in an evolving film history.

By way of the historical relationship of Dawson City to the earth below this mining town, the specific connections between the fragility of the environment and the moving image are mutually reinforced. Immediately following the excerpt from *Dawson: Gold Rush Memories* and its own narrational reflection on history, memory and impermanence, we see aerial images of the scarred landscape, filmed after the last of the region's large mines closed in 1966. The film cuts to Société Radio-Canada news footage of charred film from an archival blaze at the National Film Board of Canada's nitrate collection in 1967. Through these edits, the juxtaposition of sources and images suggests parallels across elements and ecologies and a relativism of cultures and commodities with regard to what is deemed to be a precious resource.

The environmental impact of the industrial by-products of cinema, in terms of its material base, also becomes a way of engaging other aspects of film history. For Hunter Vaughan, describing what he terms 'Hollywood's dirtiest secret', the existence of a film necessarily precedes but also succeeds its industrial applications (the distribution of a film for the duration of an exhibition cycle, for example, with Dawson City being one such end point). One must also view, he argues,

> the life cycle of the screen text through a lens that goes beyond the parameters of the typical production/distribution/exhibition assessment, considering the film's mineral prebirth, zombie remains, widescale alchemy of social design, and shelf life as tangible and symbolic object. (Vaughan 2019: 13)

This framing extends and opens up the trajectory as an historiographic or media archaeological and environmental conception,[3] as we advance towards the latter end of its cycle in the instance of the films now represented by Morrison.

Further imbricating the historical memory of Dawson City with the histories of cinema, the spectres of key industrialists and the ghosts of their

Figure 1.4 Newsreel footage of Auguste and Louis Lumière as excerpted in *Dawson City: Frozen Time*

machines are also invoked in the decaying film of *Dawson City: Frozen Time*. In one instance, by way of 1925 footage produced for Twentieth-Century Fox's *Movietone News* (Anon.), deteriorating, mottled images of French inventors and filmmakers Auguste and Louis Lumière remind us of this wider history, long after their own material contributions to cinema have entered the realm of zombie remains.

On the level of the soundtrack, beyond an elegiac contemporary score that contributes to tone and meaning, sound also functions as an audio analogue of the degradation that marks the Dawson City images. As Morrison explains the process, software was programmed to monitor the image for signs of decay and to output this visual noise as a corresponding audio signal.[4] Constituting the sonic wow to the Dawson flutter, the visual wear of the image is sonically paralleled in the form of crackle and other analogue traces (albeit digitally rendered) of the photochemical film strip.

In one instance, scenes from archival travelogues provide a phantom ride through the Yukon and its gold rush landscape. Scenes from *The Montreal Herald Screen Magazine, No. 7* (Anon., 1919) and an issue of the *Universal Screen Magazine, Vol. 1* (Anon., 1918) show an environment increasingly impacted by hydraulic mining and industrial dredging. These are images whose industrial

Figure 1.5 Damaged footage of a mined landscape as excerpted in *Dawson City: Frozen Time*

materials – light-sensitive emulsion, plasticised film strips and so on – would also be processed and discarded as Dawson City's waste. The corrosion of the image and the heavily mined landscape they depict are rendered as sonic analogue to visual noise. We hear the type of pops and crackles one might discern as a film strip's optical soundtrack is run through a projector,[5] but which might also evoke the more ominous crackle associated with the fire and flames that recur as a motif throughout *Dawson City: Frozen Time*.

Here and elsewhere, these film fragments are editorially reframed by Morrison, with additional meanings created in juxtaposition, counterpoint and other edited relations. Repurposed images take on individual and collective voices in relaying their own stories of loss and discovery by way of the new meta-narrative created through collage or assemblage. Piecing together these long-lost stories, the original narrative, newsreel and other sources are used as a structural device or formal strategy to construct interrelations and historical narrative – not just that of Dawson City or the specifics of its film archive, but of a larger cinematic history. Stories and characters are sutured across images, times and places via the vocabulary of cinema as these filmic relics assume new vitality with the ability of cinema to represent this past and reflexively recount its own history.

Alongside the use of works drawn from other archival sources, the Dawson City films are organised in such a way, for example, as to depict the gold rush that led to these films being distributed to the Yukon outpost in the first instance. Such films include *Pure Gold and Dross* (Anon., 1913) and *The End of the Rainbow* (Lynn F. Reynolds, 1916), among others.

Beyond simple thematic illustration, more complex relations are constructed. After *Dawson City: Frozen Time* recounts the discarding of countless reels of film into the Yukon River, in part via an archival newspaper headline ('Silent Pictures Dumped Into Yukon'), an intertitle from one of those films spared this very fate – only to be later buried instead – offers its own commentary. 'They threw the treasure chest overboard', proclaims *Out of the Deep* (Anon., 1912), depicting this scenario within its own narrative. Elsewhere, a montage of shots of faces expressing shock, anguish and so on represents a fictionally abstracted response to the diegetically and historically displaced narrative of Dawson City at the point of these films being buried. This is visually communicated by the title card – 'Buried Alive' – to an episode of the seemingly prescient serial *The Seven Pearls* (Louis J. Gasnier and Donald MacKenzie, 1917) and its narrative scenario that anticipated its own permafrosted fate a decade later. Onscreen text – 'The years and decades passed Dawson by' – is followed by a further montage constructed from the Dawson City films, this time depicting meta-textual slumber across a number of fictional scenarios, suggesting the extended hibernation of the archive. Later still, at the point at which *Dawson City: Frozen Time* represents the rediscovery of these films, *Out of the Deep* is reprised for further narrational illustration, by way of images of its own triumphant hunt for missing treasure.

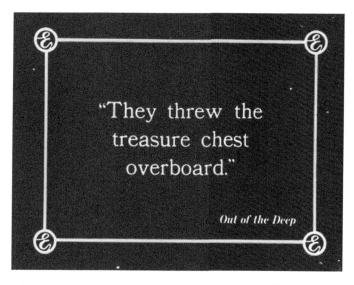

Figure 1.6 Intertitle from *Out of the Deep* as excerpted in *Dawson City: Frozen Time*

Further manipulating this footage, the formal device of the frozen image – with the moving image paused and held indefinitely – is also used on several occasions. This device constitutes its own cinematic rendering of frozen time, a visual corollary – as translated into the more typical cinematic scale of seconds rather than decades – of the temporal passage that would glaciate the Dawson City films, as well as the decades that have passed since their rediscovery in the 1970s.

The frozen image foregrounds the scales of time so central to this story and our conceptions of history (including film history), more generally. It functions not simply as punctuation but as a way to highlight the significance of individual moments and their photographic/filmic memorialisation (or their loss), and all that is implied in the distance beyond the material suspension of a historical moment. Here, André Bazin's ontological model of a 'mummy complex' is suggested in this image of life as captured by the camera and the underlying medium of film. Comparing the act of photography/cinematography to the mummification of bodies in ancient Egypt, Bazin argues, '[t]o preserve, artificially, his [a human's] bodily appearance is to snatch it from the flow of time, to stow it away neatly, so to speak, in the hold of life' (Bazin 1960 [1945]: 4–5). Such is the case with the manipulated newsreel footage of political radical Alexander Berkman. Moving images and then a still or frozen image fix his gaze towards the camera, his glance captured at the juncture of an uncertain future, at the point of his deportation from the United States in 1919. Another instance of this effect is the treatment of film footage of a legendary baseball series (the 1917 World Series, infamous for its match fixing), stopped mid-play by pausing on a still image within the newsreel, long before such play-by-play analysis would become commonplace in television sports broadcasting. Time is arrested – that is, frozen – by the photographic process, only to be animated or reanimated – unfrozen – in its subsequent projection, whether days or decades later, and whether optimally preserved in the climate-controlled conditions of a professional archival facility or in the soil of the Yukon, as in the instance of the films of Dawson City.

What emerges – from the depths beneath Dawson City and the subsequent representations of *Dawson City: Frozen Time* – is a cinema rescued from the forces of nature, archival neglect and mnemonic decay. Morrison himself suggests that

[a]s physical embodiments of social memory, and like the bits of nitrate described in the film, pushing its way through the ice, where children lit it on fire, film has the power to resurface and allow itself to be reexamined and recontextualized. (Morrison 2018)

Conversant with these contexts and histories, *Dawson City: Frozen Time* closes with a revealing, symbolic scene from *The Salamander* (Arthur Donaldson,

1916), another of those films to surface in Dawson City and thus marked forever by its geological journey. *The Salamander* tells the tale of a lizard-like creature associated with fire and capable of surviving its infernal ravages. In the footage excerpted by Morrison, an actress incarnates this mythic creature, dancing before us, in a scene now embellished by the passage of time and Dawson City's own elemental branding. The woman is engulfed by flames within the fiction, and now also by the filmic stains of water damage that seem to move as the film animates them. An intertitle from the 1916 film reminds us that '[t]he salamander of the ancients was a mythical creature that lived through fire unscorched'. Through fire as well as ice, burial as well as exhumation, cinema assumes its own mythic quality. This shot cuts to footage from *Pathé's Weekly, 17* (Anon., 1914), which also depicts a female figure in the midst of a kinetic performance as she whirls her arms and contorts her body, as if the mythical creature that has emerged from the flames is now enshrouded not by fire but by the effects of ice and the distinctive Dawson flutter.

However charred or frozen, *The Salamander* is one of the lucky ones, ultimately impervious to the conditions of neglect that saw it buried beneath the ground. In this and other examples, we are reminded of what has been lost, of the ephemerality of cinema as a medium, the neglect of photochemical film as a material base and the blind spots in our archival preservation.

In this remarkable account of physical resilience, archival perseverance and mnemonic recollection, there is a reminder of that which persists and which might emerge once more as we delve into the strata of film history. This digging is a corrective to the burial of the past – literal in the extreme case of Dawson City, but more generally, too, as we consider the abandonment of the moving image. *Dawson City: Frozen Time* depicts a cultural ecology as much as it does an environmental ecology, with memories as well as materials mined from the ground. The past can be restored to the present, however hazy, distorted and decayed, and with these markers are imprinted reminders of histories in frozen time.

CONCLUSION

Beyond Dawson City and its own geological elements and archaeological quest for film history, what might the notion of frozen time reveal about cinema and our task of accounting for its past as it exists (or does not exist) in the present? In terms of the history of a medium, how can we dig both downwards in space and backwards in time? Ultimately, in these historiographic acts, what are the cultural, archival and mnemonic legacies of cinema?

For better or worse, the traces of cinema are preserved, situating environmental materialities alongside ecologies of cultural memory. Film history is archaeologically and geologically excavated as it is literally and figuratively enacted. Photochemical film carries with it this history across time – time that is not only frozen but now thawed, melted, unfrozen. Digging into the past encourages these encounters, if only we search. Whether through the methods and metaphors of archaeology and geology, or via an environmental material-ism that treats discarded film as industrial waste as well as cultural detritus, it is possible to explore and engage the memory of a medium across a century and more.

In terms of reflexive historiography, whether self-inscriptively filmic (on the part of Morrison's cinematic meditation) or textual (on the part of this and other chapters), such discovery and its description aims to breathe new life into the cinematic corpus. It allows us to see the past in new ways, offering the potential to reframe or reimagine this history and to renegotiate our relation-ship with it from the particular perspective of today. 'If the future is endless, so is the past', suggests Morrison (cited in Jones 2017: 18), and one of the lessons of *Dawson City: Frozen Time* is that the task of the film historian is equally without bounds.

Not simply entombed or buried in the past, film history continues to live and breathe and find meaning in the present, partly as the result of a dynamic approach to history that continues to mine the past. Extending how we might apply the theoretical and historical possibilities of media archaeology, the next chapter will consider how such approaches to the moving image might be mapped not just below but above ground, too.

CHAPTER 2

A Drone's-Eye View of History: *Francofonia*

O ffering an alternative historical, technological and visual perspective, this chapter surveys a further example of a film history, one that persists in the present, creatively reconfigured or reimagined. From the earth to the ether, the focus shifts from the geological materiality of film as a medium to the physical apparatus of its imaging technologies, as we glance upwards to consider the camera-carrying drone that rises above the city of Paris in Aleksandr Sokurov's *Francofonia* (2015).

If the practices of archaeology and geology are more typically associated with a burrowing downwards into the earth, the extrapolation of a media archaeology, including Jussi Parikka's geological variation (see Parikka 2015), could include the atmosphere that surrounds the earth, encompassing an aerially borne film history. These models, for Parikka, straddle history and its metaphors, comprising both an applied archaeology of material remnants and a figurative archaeology of historical discovery. The act of unearthing, as one example, might be literal and/or figurative, an archaeology of earthly application and/or historiographic abstraction.

Similarly, as this chapter ascends into the heavens, the concept of an archaeological approach to film history operates simultaneously on multiple registers. With regard to the geological, Parikka offers a useful reminder that a geology might extend upwards, too, in terms of matter to be mined or media to be uncovered. In other words, the stratification of such a history might comprise not only that which exists below the ground, but 'a new extended geological "layer" that circles our planet' (Parikka 2015: 8). To look upwards is also to find layered connections between the histories of those imaging technologies and practices that have occupied the skies.

FRANCOFONIA: FILM HISTORY FROM ABOVE

In the instance of *Francofonia*, the play between literal and metaphorical conceptions of archaeology is explored in the historiographic realm of interrelated genealogies of aerial imaging, from cinema to war (or war to cinema), including material and other determinants of the technical design and visual aesthetics of the camera-carrying drone. This is a device that carries with it the traces of multiple histories, positioned in *Francofonia* against a broader return of the historical memory of twentieth-century war and the associated archive of filmic images and collective cultural memory of cinema.

Depicting Paris by air, both in the peacetime present and under German occupation during the Second World War, the aerial imaging of *Francofonia* places us among and above the rooftops of the city, in search of the Musée de Louvre. This is a portrait of the museum, including a reflexive concern with the very technologies of representation, the camera-carrying drone in particular. From this perspective, our vantage point is both literal (many feet in the air) and figurative (many years of flying cameras, with the drone inherently connected to the history of imaging from the air and, more complexly, a history of such imaging and its representational technologies, rooted in the practices of war). By way of this technology, as visually inscribed across a century of history in time and across the skies of a city in space, historical memory and cinematic memory are mutually mapped via an evolving apparatus, from wartime surveillance to the cinematic drone, as historical paths are retraced in the present.

Cinema's Haunted Skies

In its cinematic engagement with historical skies, *Francofonia* suggests an aerially articulated media archaeology. In this aerial archive, the drone communicates a contested history in terms of a technology that still bears its military origins and a legacy of historical conflict. As if traversing time as well as space, the use of the drone transports history, including film history, into the present. Its images illustrate not only the world below but a history of aerial imaging whose cumulative lineage is embodied in its forms and functions and aesthetically inscribed in its movements and images. Put simply: in *Francofonia*, the drone tells its own tale.

More generally, placing this concern with film history in a wider historical context, on the level of subject matter and theme, *Francofonia* returns us to the Paris of the Second World War, with a particular emphasis on the Louvre and its artistic treasures at the point of occupation by the German army in June 1940. The occupation followed the declaration of Paris as a so-called open city – so designated in order to spare damage to life as well as property. In particular peril was the irreplaceable cultural heritage of the Louvre, which was in danger of being plundered in the name of *Kunstschutz* (art protection). The designation of open city would serve to protect Paris, partly in order for its precious artefacts to be spirited away from German occupiers. In *Francofonia*, this focus on the museum in the midst of such conflict serves as the starting point for a cinematic meditation on European history (indeed, the tagline of the film is

'An Elegy for Europe'), the memory of war and the place of art and its preservation as sites of civilisation within the dynamics of shifting geopolitics and
imperial conquest.

To this list of concerns we might add aerial imaging itself, including cinematography. In depicting the Paris of the Louvre, *Francofonia* envisions a
view not only of the museum, but of a history (or pre-history) of the drone,
as Sokurov launches his own camera-equipped device to channel mnemonic
and archival traces of the past. This is a history both troubled and troubling, a
flyover of aerial imaging technologies, from the military past to the cinematic
present, with particular parallels and antecedence in aerial photographic reconnaissance – of Paris as well as countless other cities, across the skies of Western
Europe – during the Second World War. This historical imaging is reprised in
the drone's depiction of contemporary Paris. While relatively few in number,
the instances of drone footage in *Francofonia* – several lengthy shots, photographed by Bruno Delbonnel – are nevertheless a key element of the film and
its depiction of Paris.

On the level of form, as a framework in which these drone-captured
images operate, *Francofonia* combines archival footage (of wartime Paris
and its German occupiers, for example), newly shot footage (of Paris, most
notably the Louvre) and contemporary footage that is artificially manipulated in a variety of ways to give the impression of the archival and historical
(such as dramatic recreations that are sepia-tinted and otherwise processed
or enhanced). The overall approach is a reflexive use of comparative imaging
and visual effects across a number of technologies that draws attention to its
own artifice and manipulations of time, memory and historicity, and their
signification.

This relationship between the realms of political history and film history is
simultaneously a combination of historical memory (in this instance, the legacy
of war as waged in continental Europe) and cinematic memory (the history of
a medium, including its imaging technologies), historical trauma (the scars of
the Second World War) and cinematic trauma (fundamental challenges to its
representational modes), albeit on very different scales and with very different
stakes or consequences.

For Marijeta Bozovic, describing these dynamics, *Francofonia* is a film
'[h]aunted alike by visual technologies and an obsessive return to the epicenter
of modern European trauma, World War II' (Bozovic 2016). In this sense, a
certain corollary is drawn between the history of Europe and that of cinema, as
mediated in and via its technologies of representation. The drone functions, in
this respect, in the context of a broader engagement with visual technologies
that are elegiac, seemingly haunted, whether by the past or by other ghosts in
the machine.

The drone, in particular, is one such visual technology – haunted, in Bozovic's terms – in its connections to airborne antecedents and camera-carrying precursors with regard to prior technologies whose principal imaging is derived from military applications and other types of reconnaissance and surveillance.

Specifically, prior to the proliferation of the drone as a commercial, recreational and cinematic device, its history as a tool of aerial imaging of one kind or another, via one device or another, has its origins in military contexts and applications. This history encompasses a number of devices, from balloons to aeroplanes and on towards the more recent iteration of the unmanned aerial vehicle – more commonly known as the drone – whether armed or unarmed, intended purely to surveil or to attack.[1]

Indeed, it is only in recent years that such imaging has been adapted from the militaristic to the cinematic. The drone has become increasingly prevalent within cinema, both in its explicit use as an element of visual spectacle and as a more invisible device used to carry the camera in lieu of dollies, cranes and other jibs and rigs. The drone has entered the technical apparatus as well as the aesthetic lexicon of cinema, since it has become a consumer as well as industrial imaging device.

At the same time, this technology retains its application as well as legacy of conflict, including as historically contextualised and formally elucidated in *Francofonia*, in a past that continues to leave aesthetic traces and retain mnemonic resonance in the present. Cinema holds the capacity to articulate such history on the level of form, rooted in its technologies and their aesthetic operations. This includes the underlying apparatus, both as the source of an archive of images and as technical objects, imbued with material histories that might communicate their own memorial significance.

For instance, in footage presumably filmed from the air by drone, *Francofonia* documents images of the streets and rooftops of Paris, as well as glimpses of the Louvre itself. The camera moves through a narrow Parisian street, ascending from the rooftops onwards, upwards and skywards. Once the drone is significantly elevated, the vast expanse of the sprawling Parisian cityscape comes into view, stretching into the beyond. The drone and its camera continue their trajectory before the airborne camera tilts downwards to film the streets directly below while the drone moves laterally. The film cuts to a shot of a clapperboard, labelled for a production entitled 'Francofonia', presumably the very film we now watch.

'A people is surrounded by an ocean, while a person has his ocean within', notes *Francofonia*'s narrator, Aleksandr, voiced by Aleksandr Sokurov himself, over the drone shot as the camera glides ethereally through and above the streets of Paris in order to capture its aerial views. 'Is the camera already rolling?' the narrator continues as the drone roams, a reflexive ruse combined with the subsequent sonic clap of the clapperboard. 'Then let's go . . .'

Figures 2.1–2.2 Tilting drone shot of the Parisian skyline (top) and rooftops (bottom) in *Francofonia*

But 'let's go' where? And how? After all, not all means of navigating a city are equal, nor are the means of representing this navigation. The emphasis on metaphorical seas that surround, as the camera soars above the cityscape as ocean, is a reminder of the unique ability of the drone to conquer space. Time and space in individual experience expands, and its meta-physical ocean within connects to the meta-historical ocean without. In this extended movement, the drone choreographs an out-of-body, out-of-city and out-of-time experience.

In authorial terms, with regard to how the camera articulates space, one could draw comparisons between the approximately ninety-minute single Steadicam shot of Sokurov's *Russian Ark* (*Russkiy kovcheg*, 2002), and the more extensively untethered drone camerawork of *Francofonia*. Indeed, there are obvious parallels between these formal strategies or aesthetic devices, including the aforementioned metaphor of sailing upon an ocean or oceans of history, and the very particular focus in each of these films on exploring history as collected within the museum as a site of antiquity and nationhood, culture and memory – the State Hermitage Museum in the Saint Petersburg of *Russian Ark* and the Louvre in the Paris of *Francofonia*.

A more apt comparison might be to a film such as Haroun Farocki's *Images of the World and the Inscription of War* (*Bilder der Welt und Inschrift des Krieges*, 1989), with its historical focus on aerial imaging whose surveillance unintentionally documents and thus evidences certain atrocities of the Holocaust that occurred on the ground below. After all, the ascent in the shift from Steadicam in *Russian Ark* to drone in *Francofonia* also implicates and consciously invokes a visual history of aerial surveillance, from photographic reconnaissance to the remote-controlled drone. Specifically, as *Francofonia* reminds us, the aerial camera has long been a device of war, and its military origins remain palpable, even in the filming of contemporary Paris. Farocki's film likewise maps the imaging apparatuses of war and the perspectival shifts associated with the inscription of the world – including the most profound of human scars – from the air, whether by photograph, cinema or other airborne means.

Sokurov links the technologies of aerial representation via drone to our mediated perception of history and geography, cinema and war. In its contemporary aerial manoeuvres, in a film about a historical Paris, *Francofonia* implicitly connects the aerial imaging of the past (including the wartime Europe depicted in the film) and the aerial imaging of the present. The drone as apparatus becomes a locus of memory, including the prior history of this very technology.

From Cinema to War and Back Again

Military applications during the Second World War brought cinema and war into a heightened dialogue, visually mediated by the shared apparatus of the camera. Although separated by historical distance and design, there is a clear trajectory from the aerial photo-reconnaissance missions flown by various air forces during the Second World War and the camera-equipped drones that have entered the cinematic apparatus. As comparatively contextualised and imaged in *Francofonia*, the drone parallels the aerial cinematography (alongside the more common still photography) of those specially equipped aeroplanes that flew over the skies of Paris and other cities during the Second World War as a means to scout and surveil, seeking visual intelligence of one kind or another, as the functional and aesthetic precursors to the drone of today.

In these multiple genealogies, what is now cinematic was once militaristic, across the respective demands to represent and surveil. Indeed, as Catherine Zimmer argues in her study of surveillance more generally, '[t]he visual technologies associated with cinema are intimately connected with surveillance practice and the production of knowledge through visibility' (Zimmer 2015: 4).

The drone, and its representations, are linked in turn to what Paul Virilio terms 'The Logistics of Perception', the subtitle of his seminal work, *War and Cinema*. First published in 1984, it predates the contemporary cinematic drone, yet charts an earlier history of aerial cinematography as common to both cinema and war. For Virilio, imaging from the air has been inseparable from military engagements over the last century, not least the aerial imaging of the First and Second World Wars, charting a history by which 'aerial reconnaissance, both tactical and strategic, became chronophotographic and then cinematographic' (Virilio 1989 [1984]: 17–18). During the latter of these wars, he argues,

> [t]he extreme mobility of mechanized armies imparted a new temporal unity that only cinema could apprehend, albeit with occasional difficulty since the greater speed of aircraft extended the flow of images and high altitudes iced up the camera's mechanism. [. . .]
> The limits of investigation, in both time and space, were being pushed back. (Virilio 1989 [1984]: 74–5)

In the years since, pushing back even farther, cinematic drones – derived from what Mike McConnell describes as 'flying, high resolution video cameras armed with missiles' (cited in Chamayou 2015 [2013]: 12) – represent a further manifestation of this trajectory, including Virilio's famous maxim that '[w]ar is cinema and cinema is war' (Virilio 1989 [1984]: 26).[2]

Virilio outlines what Friedrich Kittler would later describe as 'the historically perfect collusion of world wars, reconnaissance squadrons, and cinematography' (Kittler 1999 [1986]: 124), emphasising again the relationship between mediated warfare and cinema. In presenting a parallel history of camera and gun, including elements of shared technology, Kittler details the related applications and even interchangeability of these devices in aerial usage, such as cameras deployed alongside or instead of a weapon, with an aeroplane equipped to shoot – in both senses of the word – during flight. Camera technology and automatic weaponry coincide in a number of ways, across this shared history.

For example, Beaumont Newhall writes that during the Second World War, the reconnaissance image was considered so vital – including to the German Luftwaffe over France – that it was often prioritised above more direct forms of combat. Dedicated photographic reconnaissance 'planes carried no guns', he explains.

> They were unarmed not only to decrease their weight and thus to increase their speed and range [. . .] but also to remove the pilot's temptation to engage in combat at the expense of securing photographs. His only defense was speed, and his orders were to run away from planes attempting to intercept him. (Newhall 1969: 57)

With the camera mounted to the underside of an aeroplane, the role of the human pilot was to chart a path that would allow for optimal imaging from the air.

Whether deployed as a camera for capturing moving images, or adapted to operate as a high-capacity photographic camera for individual or serial still images, the film camera was a central tool in this effort to visualise from above. Outlining the adaptation of film cameras for still and serial photographic uses, Roy M. Stanley explains how '[a]utomatic cameras were developed by upscaling and modifying movie camera technology – thus the name *Reihenbilder* ("series pictures"), which gave an "Rb" prefix to most subsequent German aerial cameras' (Stanley 1981: 172). Still photographic cameras were used alongside these specially adapted film cameras, whose larger magazine capacity allowed for more images to be captured on a single reconnaissance mission. Film cameras were also sometimes used in their original capacity, to capture moving images as opposed to intermittent or serial still images.

Any city could be documented from the air, as Paris is in *Francofonia*, not by camera-carrying aeroplanes, but by the contemporary variant of such aerial photography, the camera-carrying drone. Immediately prior to one such shot in the film, we see the skies above a sepia-toned Louvre, filmed in the present (*c*.2015) but processed using visual effects to give the impression of age (*c*.1940), as German planes – perhaps, in this CGI fantasy, equipped with their own photographic devices – fly overhead by way of Sokurov's visual effects.

As these CGI-enabled aeroplanes chart their trans-historical and trans-technological paths, the film cuts to a similarly sepia-toned shot, this time via drone, depicting a decidedly present-day Louvre as contemporary patrons wander its exterior and modern cars drive by. We, too, are now visitors to the Louvre, courtesy of the cinematic drone that passes through an archway and on towards the museum, slowly rising as it advances through the grounds.

Establishing further historical relations, this contemporary drone footage is intercut with archival footage of aerial wartime operations: a shot of the lifting wheels and undercarriage of a German aeroplane on take-off in its own trajectory of ascent, more than seventy years earlier, followed by a shot of a pilot in flight as he glances outwards to conduct his own visual surveillance.

One final shot in this sequence of aerial technologies – and, in their realisation, imaging technologies, too – depicts a further flight, this time within the Louvre, as a surreal scenario occurs before the camera. In a dimly lit interior courtyard of the museum, in a play with time, space and the technological illusion of cinema, a Luftwaffe aeroplane circa the Second World War appears to glide slowly through the museum itself, propellers whirring. It is, of course, an improbable image for all sorts of reasons, created only through trickery, playful in its visual construction of the historical dynamics of the museum as a disputed site during the period of occupation. In terms of cinema, meanwhile, the aeroplane that glides within the space of the museum is not unlike the drone's own ability to glide through the air, precisely as it does in the previous shots that guide us towards the Louvre in the first instance.

The technologies in the film (CGI Luftwaffe aeroplanes, which fly above a Louvre filmed in the present but sepia-tinted to give the impression of age; the camera-carrying drone that offers its own flight in guiding us ever closer to the museum in the present; the film camera attached to a wartime aeroplane; and, within the museum itself, the gliding aeroplane, *c*.1940, yet visualised in the present) are each capable of aerial imaging. This deployment encourages a contextual or comparative reading of respective technologies, modes and eras. The implied relations across these images bridge technologies and temporalities, suggesting a historical context for the film's contemporary footage of Paris, first, and its means or technologies of representation, second. That is, the edit connects aerial imaging of past and present alongside the further comparative imaging and reflexive historiography of the CGI-augmented skies above the Louvre and the Luftwaffe aeroplane that enters the courtyard of the museum.

The drone carries with it the forms, functions and, to a certain extent, hardwired technology of the past; it carries with it, too, the resonances of a history of images captured from the air, now placed in historical dialogue via Sokurov's editing and other strategies.

In another example of the use of drone footage in *Francofonia*, historical continuities, technologically and aesthetically mediated, are further invoked in images that visually communicate their own historicity. In a shot of approximately a minute in duration, the drone-borne camera manoeuvres the narrow streets of Paris, as Sokurov, again in voiceover, describes the designation of Paris as an open city. Recalling the historical shadow of the context of war, this

Figures 2.3–2.6 Comparative technologies in *Francofonia* in the form of CGI aeroplanes (top), a shot captured by drone (middle, upper), footage filmed from an aeroplane (middle, lower), the illusion of an aeroplane within the Musée du Louvre (bottom)

shot, in turn, is juxtaposed with archival footage of the city's streets, a historical relationship marked in thematic and graphic relations across shots, as well as in the distinction between black-and-white (past) and colour (present) and the mediating technology of the static film camera (past) and camera-equipped drone (present).

In this instance, the drone is not at high altitude, rather the relatively low altitude of near street level. The drone and its camera make their way at a height of tens rather than hundreds of feet in the air, and at times seem to be barely inches from the facades of the buildings they pass to the left and right.

At the shot's opening, as if to play with the spectator's mediated sense of history and invite direct comparison between past and present, Sokurov bridges the cut from an archival scene of wartime Paris (specifically, of French troops returning home from combat) with the drone's navigation of the Paris streets of today, artificially desaturating the first few seconds of this contemporary drone footage before gradually restoring colour. For a brief moment, we are placed in a historical no-man's land, somewhere between the Paris of the 1940s and that of today, via a visual shorthand signifier of the past (the greyscale image) conjoined with the gliding movement through the air that has become characteristic of the drone's cinematic present. The black-and-white to colour transition, from archival past to drone-drenched present, invites further comparison: for example, between the ethereal images of the city in a time of peace, and the role of aerial imaging in a time of war.

Paradoxically, this camera-eye as machine of war is also capable of physical and aesthetic transcendence: weightless, smooth and fluid, producing an effect or sensation that led one reviewer to describe *Francofonia* in terms of its 'amazing drone-captured visuals of Paris from low altitudes' (Roeper 2016).

As this particular drone shot ends, the film cuts to further archival footage of occupied Paris. In a thematic as well as graphic match of the footage filmed by drone, we cut from the balcony windows of a Parisian residence in the present to a similar scene and composition in wartime, of a woman opening and peering from her own shuttered windows. Again, moments in time overlap one another in a visualised slippage of historical, cultural and cinematic memory, as technologically rendered. The drone hovers – literally and figuratively – at the boundaries between cinema, war and representation, moving us backwards and forwards in time as we witness the same balcony-lined streets, but in different eras and via different devices.

Here and elsewhere, in its aerial manoeuvres, the drone of *Francofonia* connects past and present: Paris under German occupation and the city as liberated; war and its memory; a military technology and its civilian incarnations; an archive of filmic images and a contemporary cinema in dialogue with this history – a history now aerially borne, aesthetically inscribed and reflexively revealed.

Figures 2.7–2.8 The streets of Paris depicted in contemporary (top) and archival (bottom) footage in *Francofonia*

CONCLUSION

Regarding imaging technologies, we might ask – and, indeed, are encouraged to ask in these thematic parallels and formal relations – what connects the cameras of the German reconnaissance aeroplanes of the Second World War with

Sokurov's cinematic drone of today? How does this technology embody and inscribe its own traumatic history, rooted in modern warfare? And, ultimately, what might we glean from this aerial survey of history – not least, film history – by way of our drone-enabled position high above the Louvre? In *Francofonia*'s aerial imaging, we peer upon not only the historical skies of Paris, but the evolving history of cinema and its underlying technologies, as the past appears in the skies of the present.

In the instance of the aerial photo-reconnaissance of the Second World War, to capture images from the air was just one part of a representational equation, which also required specialist interpretation. Such analysis was necessitated by the altered perspective of seeing the world from above. Indeed, as Newhall describes this process of visual adjustment,

> [t]he techniques of photo interpretation are simple: the careful comparison of photo coverage over days, weeks and even months; the use of stereo vision; the measurement of images to the tenth part of a millimeter with a high-power magnifier fitted with a graticule; and, above all, visual imagination. (Newhall 1969: 63)

Decades later, and applied to the moving rather than the still image and as captured not by aeroplane but by drone, what do we see, and what might we interpret, as we look upon the Paris of *Francofonia* with, above all, visual imagination?

Imaging from the air allows a landscape or topography to be seen in new ways. It can also give us the benefit of a metaphorical as well as literal reframing. As Caren Kaplan has observed in her own detailed history of aerial imaging, '[a]rtifacts of distance like aerial images' (Kaplan 2018: 216) exist in ways that reimagine the everyday, suggesting new ways of seeing and thinking across senses, dimensions and periods. She continues elsewhere:

> If we consider that they are always already connecting us to places and times at a distance from us, we may become sensitive to other possibilities – places, times, people, living and inanimate things. Aerial views make possible and impossible the arts of war in unfolding aftermaths – worlding and unworlding, disturbing the peace. (Kaplan 2018: 216)

As the airborne camera, elevated by a drone, rises above Paris, it carries with it countless years of cumulative history. Against a backdrop of the continuing legacy of twentieth-century war, the cine-historiography of *Francofonia* helps us place the drone within the history of aerial imaging and consider the resonant historicity of contemporary cinema. Once more, cinema is reframed, visually and historically, with the altered visual perspective afforded by the aerial optics of the drone's camera, with a means to navigate the history of film: Paris by air, film history from above.

If, as Steen Ledet Christiansen argues, '[c]ontemporary cinema is entering the drone age' (Christiansen 2017: 1), this cinema has largely effaced the military origins of this technology, even while embracing the visual aesthetics and spectacle at its core. In an era in which the cinematic drone has become near ubiquitous, it has also been abstracted as a visual trope, shorn of history and signification. In this surfeit of drone images, the militarised uses of this technology, as well as the aerial imaging technologies that preceded contemporary applications of the drone, have been dehistoricised and depoliticised.

By contrast, in its engagement with this technology and historical memory, filmic and otherwise, *Francofonia* represents a reflexive use of the drone, atypical of much of contemporary cinema in its self-awareness. Put another way, it foregrounds those properties of the drone that are more typically invisible in popular generic contexts but are inherent within it and its associated aesthetics, embedded in its technics and design and inscribed as abstracted traces of the past in its visual representations of the present.

In depicting the history of Paris, *Francofonia* features the skies above the city as a conflicted celestial perspective on a terrestrial landscape historically divided and contained by war. With his emphasis on the Louvre, situated within the context of the German pursuit of French art, Sokurov engages the fundamental contradiction – the freedom of unfettered movement and ocular expansion versus the strictures of that which is surveilled or occupied – in a history of violence that is typically denied, hidden or erased by other means. *Francofonia* acknowledges this past, implicitly revealing the political and other histories inherent to the drone.

Sokurov himself has spoken of the vectors of history more generally, saying that '[o]nly a great work of art has the capacity to link the past to the future and the present' (cited in Gray 2015). With regard to *Francofonia*, in particular, producer Pierre-Olivier Bardet suggests that

> [t]he film features many ghosts, of which there are many in the Louvre alongside its paintings. [. . .] For Aleksandr [Sokurov] the past is not something which is behind us, it is something that is under our feet – you just need to dig to find it. (Cited in Wiseman 2015)

The past is indeed under our feet, as we float in the air by way of the camera-carrying drone. Art and history are inseparable, for Sokurov. War and cinema are inseparable, for Virilio, Kittler and others. As the drone, as a technological affordance, and the drone shot, as its visual inscription, assume a cine-historical dimension, cinema's past and present are inseparable, too.

Its technologies convey their own mediated memories, cinema's own haunted pasts, into the present and beyond. In *Francofonia*, we glide, hover and fly above Paris in part because the Luftwaffe – like countless other militaries elsewhere, then and since – charted its own filmic paths above Paris nearly eighty years ago. Cinema, in this drone's-eye view, becomes also an example of déjà vu.

CHAPTER 3

The Movie Theatre as Haunted Space: *Shirin* and *70×70*

This chapter focuses on the historical resonance of the movie theatre as a haunted space, inhabited by the memory of a medium and the cumulative history of more than a century of projected cinema. Even while films are streamed, downloaded and otherwise consumed like never before,[1] the particular confluence of projector, screen, film and spectator has assumed altered meaning, mapped in time and space, across physical and psychic histories and geographies. The cinematic experience has been transformed, ontologically, phenomenologically and historically – as symbol, spectre and trace.

Seminal works such as Roland Barthes's 'Leaving the Movie Theater' (Barthes 1986 [1975]) and the individual phenomenology of moviegoing described in Stanley Cavell's *The World Viewed: Reflections on the Ontology of Film* (1971) offer illuminating models of engaging the particular architecture of the movie theatre and for theorising the act of spectatorship. Nevertheless, they no longer adequately account for a time in which the projection of a film within a movie theatre and the primacy of such sites recedes into history, assuming altered historicity in the process. Ghostliness, spectrality and what Jacques Derrida describes as 'hauntology' (Derrida 1994 [1993]), part of a broader spectral turn, reflect the experience of seeing and hearing a film in a site whose increasing obsolescence has come to represent the fleeting and ephemeral, notions that have become an increasingly important part of how we historicise cinema. The movie theatre exists as a site of spatialised media archaeology, the symbol of a medium defined simultaneously by its presence and absence, a material apparatus and its negation, embodied experience and its recollection.

Spanning consecutive case studies across countries and modes, the chapter begins with a single screening as an exploration of the technology, architecture and site-specific cartographies of spectatorial affect, real or illusory, in the reflexive representations of Abbas Kiarostami's *Shirin* (2008). It then considers the interconnected network of a life's worth of such screenings as documented by Iain Sinclair in his curatorial project and cinematic memoir *70×70: Unlicensed Preaching: A Life Unpacked in 70 Films* (2014). In each of these instances of experimental historiography, the emphasis is on the legacy and historical (re-)enactment of cinema as projected experience, a means of exploring and documenting the movie theatre as a still resonant site and space of shared history and cultural memory.

In grappling with these ideas, the following questions arise: How, in historical terms, might we account for the changing status of the movie theatre as a symbolic locus for the memory of a medium? In mapping histories of cinema, what value should we place on the spectral (rather than material), the hauntological (rather than ontological) and the psychogeographic (rather than geographic)? And, ultimately, how might we usefully engage the resonance of such cinematic encounters without lapsing into nostalgia?

SHIRIN: CINEMA AS REFLEXIVE REVENANT

> Once upon a time, most people could only watch a movie in the cinema where it was projected at the correct pace for the illusion of movement and according to a given narrative sequence.
>
> – Laura Mulvey (Mulvey 2006: 21–2)

> The ultimate goal of film history is an account of its own disappearance, or its transformation into another entity.
>
> – Paolo Cherchi Usai (Cherchi Usai 2001: 89)

Engaging shifts in film culture that continue to play out today, *Shirin* explores the changing status of cinema – not least, the cinematic experience – in its most symbolic of sites and modes of exhibition, the projection of films to an audience within a movie theatre. Considered in relation to hauntology, the film's representation of the movie theatre as haunted space, and its audience as spectral spectators, can be analysed as potent signifiers of a medium in existential transition.

Specifically, *Shirin* represents and articulates the physical and symbolic contours of the interior of a movie theatre, in which an unknown film is seemingly projected for an audience whose faces and reactions are documented in the midst of the spectatorial act. *Shirin* is far from the first film to depict the space of the movie theatre, but placed in broader historical context, it exemplifies a decidedly reflexive interrogation. On one level, *Shirin* is about cinema as a site-specific experience, one that predominated for decades but whose representation today reminds us of its disappearance – or at least its displacement. At the same time, *Shirin*'s movie theatre is also an environment that evokes the 'spectre' in Derrida's terms (1994 [1993]), of not only a site-specific experience, but an entire medium – cinema – and its postulated death. The movie theatre becomes a site to celebrate the history of a medium, and also to mourn and memorialise its passing. In this respect, *Shirin* constructs an allegory of our relationship with cinema and its history. Channelling one historical era into another, the film engages and relocates the increasingly absent or invisible theatrical cinema, rendering it visible once more, yet via the spectrality of a summoning into a time and place where this cinematic experience no longer fully belongs. Conjuring the cinematic experience of a prior era in the context of a reconfigured technological and cultural landscape, a space is opened up for a visit from this ghostly revenant.

Positing how we might engage this sense of history, *Shirin* bypasses the potential reductiveness of pure nostalgia or a conception of the demise – if that is what it is – of a medium as a precisely delineated finitude. Instead, *Shirin* complicates its vision of cinema and the cinematic experience via a series of reflexive strategies that challenge the representational status of the cinematic image in a complex negotiation of present and past, presence and absence, ontology and hauntology. Consistent with the broader authorial concerns of director Kiarostami's work, and as a variation on the spectrality and mourning that Derrida identifies as central to the hauntological resonance of a 'thing itself' (Derrida 1994 [1993]: 10), this representation of cinema and its history is one that interrogates the status of the very object that is mourned and the very process of mourning.

In these theoretical, historical and historiographic contexts, the movie theatre of *Shirin* can be understood as a symbolic landscape – a site of media archaeological ghosts that gather in the palace of dreams. The landscape invites reflection on the status of cinema and its sites of exhibition and modes of spectatorship at a time when movie theatres and audiences of the type represented in *Shirin* continue to recede into history, and when cinema itself might be considered a historical cultural form.

Hauntology and Historiography

Encompassing conceptions of death and that which comes after, *Shirin* negotiates a broader historical context in which the projection of films in a movie theatre has become an increasingly niche experience, and in which cinema itself, for many, exists only post-mortem.[2] To represent the movie theatre today, and to reflect on the nature of cinema, as *Shirin* does, is to negotiate a historical moment in which cinema's past and present exist, to a certain extent, out of phase. That is, if the past continues to bear meaning in the present, evoking a history and collective experience of cinema, it is as a haunting that expresses a sense of loss, memory and nostalgia. In this context, the model of hauntology offers one way of conceptualising this spectre, a means of understanding and historicising the ghost of cinema, which continues to haunt, and whose spectrality is conjured and explored by *Shirin*.

Shirin embodies a spectre of the very passing of cinema – or at least a certain experience of cinema: a film projected within the darkened space of the movie theatre. Where projected cinema continues to exist, it is as an imitation of the moviegoing culture and mass visibility it once held, or as a historical recreation, acutely aware of its history and historicity.

Shirin inhabits the historiographic – and hauntological – realm that Stephen Barber describes as '[f]ilm's post-death ghostworld' (Barber 2010: 27), in that it engages cinema precisely in the wake of a decades-long debate concerning its death, including discussion of the erosion (or evolution) of a general culture of cinephilia as well as the transformed technologies, contexts and cultures that have supplanted the primacy of the movie theatre, and of moviegoing.

In this context, as mediated by *Shirin*, the movie theatre has assumed new meaning. For many, it remains a revered, privileged space in which to experience a film, an idealised conception that is clung to or even amplified, as if in denial – or precisely because – of fundamental technological and other shifts. Such notions are rooted in what Thomas Elsaesser calls *the love that never lies* (cinephilia as the love of the original, of authenticity, of the indexicality of time, where each film performance is a unique event)' (Elsaesser 2005: 41), referring to a historical culture that privileges a certain type of 'going to the movies' (Elsaesser 2005: 29), a notion that has persisted in recent years, even in the midst of its potential obsolescence. As Cherchi Usai writes, '[t]he impending demise of cinema [. . .] is announced by a belated *coup de théâtre*. Soon after being declared on the verge of extinction, film acquired a new cultural status and was given the red carpet treatment' (Cherchi Usai 2011: 60).

Regardless, as Cherchi Usai acknowledges in his description of 'demise', the movie theatre has also become the symbolic locus for what Mulvey describes as a 'resonance of ageing, and of death' (Mulvey 2006: 18), and which Francesco Casetti frames in terms of a broader context in which '[c]inema remains with us [. . .] But its survival is also marked with the sense of death, if only as a reflection of the fear that it could indeed disappear' (Casetti 2015: 14). The movie theatre – no longer the movie palace of implied grandeur – has become a graveyard or mausoleum, a memorial or site of remembrance, both a site of mourning and a site to be mourned. For Barber, '[w]hat remains of cinema is abandoned: abandoned images, abandoned buildings, together with a volatile set of traces compacted from memory, obsession, corporeality, imagination, excess, and sensory responses and impacts' (Barber 2010: 29), in what he describes as a 'revealing terrain of cinematic abandonment' (Barber 2010: 8), a landscape that comprises nothing less than 'ghost-spaces' (Barber 2010: 18).

To represent the movie theatre as such a space, as *Shirin* does, is to engage with the spectral or simulacral dimensions of the medium, wherein, according to Caetlin Benson-Allott, 'the cinema itself has become simulacral, a phantasm that no longer refers to any actual film culture but only conjures the cultural or economic capital of one' (Benson-Allott 2013: 133). The movie theatre and the cinematic experience associated with it, has assumed not only altered meaning, but altered status, in terms of the significance of this space as one of vitality in the present.

Not only as a site of continuing collective experience, but as a function of collective cultural memory, the movie theatre has increasingly become historic, a physical environment that embodies a century or more of memories. In the cinematic representation of this space lives a desire to remember, an attachment to a golden age – real or imagined – that no longer fully exists, but which continues to resonate in the present. More than ever, the movie theatre has become a symbolic site that evokes traces and fragments of past experiences now embedded in a collective mnemonic archive. Described another way, the movie theatre has become a haunted – or hauntological – space, in which the act of collective cinematic spectatorship has become a haunted – or hauntological – gaze.

If, for Derrida, hauntology first referred to the 'specters of Marx' (1994 [1993]), which Derrida argued would haunt Western society from beyond the grave, this concept might also inform our understanding of cinema in its contemporary incarnations. Derrida's spectre is not a ghost in any supernatural sense, rather a simulacral virtuality, something that exists or is manifest in the present without physical incarnation.

For example, beyond the spectral vestiges of Marxism, hauntology also offers a means of conceptualising an end-of-history uncanniness, wherein new technologies, among other factors, have challenged traditional understandings of time and place. In the context of cinema, and as represented by a film such as *Shirin*, it is not typically Marxism that haunts an ontologically reoriented cinema, but the very memory of cinema itself, including the movie theatre and the distinctive phenomenology associated with this site.

Indeed, with regard to historicity, the preternatural persistence of the past into the present, which *Shirin* represents, is one such example. Hauntology typically occurs in two types of historical overlap: a past that lingers into the present beyond its original ontology or historical moment in one direction, and a future that is born too early into a present that has yet to bestow it the material presence and meaning of ontology in the other. As Mark Fisher further delineates:

> The first refers to that which is (in actuality is) *no longer*, but which is still effective as a virtuality (the traumatic 'compulsion to repeat', a structure that repeats, a fatal pattern). The second refers to that which

(in actuality) has *not yet* happened, but which is *already* effective in the virtual (an attractor, an anticipation shaping current behavior). (Fisher 2012: 19)

It is the first of these two scenarios – the virtuality of a compulsively returned to no longer – that is most marked in *Shirin*, as well as the broader context of the altered ontology it negotiates. As D. N. Rodowick has observed, '[f]or the time being, theatrical cinema is our passing present, our disappearing ontology. But this also means that it is not yet completely past, and that the emergent future may remain, for some time to come, cinematic' (Rodowick 2007: 93). In a concurrent disappearing and emerging, a potential ontological/hauntological slippage arises, a cinematic spectre that might inhabit the space that exists between these states.

In this intersection of historiography and hauntology – in cinema and in *Shirin* – the question is not Derrida's '[w]hither Marxism?' (Derrida 1994 [1993]: 9), nor even Rodowick's '[w]hat *was* cinema?' (Rodowick 2007: 25–87),[3] but how might we locate cinema, or its ghost, at a time of ontological/ hauntological transition? Put simply: Whither cinema?

The (Negated) Screen and the (Spectral) Spectator

Addressing one such quest for the cinematic, ghostly or otherwise, in the realm of representation that exists beyond narrative, Kiarostami proposes that we 'watch another world which is more attractive than the story. I believe if you dare let go of the story, you will come across a new thing which is the Cinema itself' (cited in Khodaei 2009). If Kiarostami exhorts us to let go of the story, to seek nothing less than the cinema itself, how might we define cinema at this moment in history? Beyond a simple determination of death or a historiographic delineation of existential demise, what new status, meaning and signification has the site of the movie theatre and the practice of moviegoing assumed?

In *Shirin*, it is precisely cinema and its history that come to the fore as its own subject, divorced from conventional storytelling. This is not a narrative in any straightforward sense but instead a reflexive or meta-cinematic experience in which, for the duration of its approximately ninety minutes, we witness what *appears* to be an audience who in turn watch what *appears* to be a film – that is, a film-within-the-film – one that we never see, but which we hear from beginning to end, bookended by the opening and closing credits of *Shirin*.

In many respects, this concern with the nature of cinema is an extension of the modernist authorial concerns of Kiarostami,[4] whose oeuvre consistently explores our attachment to narrative and illusionism by creating instead what Mulvey describes as a 'cinema of uncertainty' (Mulvey 2006: 123–43), a filmmaking that resides in and consciously explores 'the distance between a reality and its representation' (Mulvey 2006: 128), including those 'absences in representation that are usually displaced by the needs of an externally determined system of ordering, such as narrational coherence' (Mulvey 2006: 125). For François Fronty, identifying one such displacement, *Shirin* 'is not an invitation to exegeses. It offers a direct, polysemic reading not only of the text and the film, but of cinema itself' (Fronty 2009: 82).

In order to go beyond the text and the film to the cinema, the spectator of *Shirin* must first transcend the absence of underlying visual input, the thing we expect most from a film (if we can even call the film-within-the-film a film, given that we never actually see it). The underlying story is a retelling of a work by twelfth-century Persian poet Nizami Ganjavi. 'Khosrow and Shirin' (Khusraw u Shirin) is a tragic melodrama of a love triangle between a Persian king, Khosrow, an Armenian princess, Shirin, and an alternative suitor for the love of Shirin, Farhad, which the eponymous Shirin narrates to a group of women at the site of her lover's death by suicide before she, too, takes her own life.

While we hear a soundtrack (ostensibly, a conventional mix of music, sound effects and dialogue) to the apparent film-within-the-film, we experience its story visually only in relief or by proxy, via the reactions of what appears to be an audience of moviegoers composed principally of women. The visual and the aural are separated from one another; we do not see what we assume the women to be seeing, but we hear what we assume them to be hearing. The story of the film-within-the-film is thus told, in large part, through shots of the faces of these women as we follow their reactions across the emotional register as they appear to watch this epic historical melodrama.

As spectators, we are invited to gaze at a succession of static shots of these subjects, in close-up or medium close-up – figures who are sometimes alone, at other times in groups of two, three or four. Close framing focuses our gaze on head and shoulders, allowing us to look directly at the faces and observe the changing expressions of subjects in a spectatorial reverie. We watch these reactions to the drama that appears to unfold via a screen that remains beyond our view. The foregrounded subjects are exclusively women,[5] though we also see male spectators in the background. Over the course of the film, we witness more than 100 such women (the closing credits list a total of 110 names under the heading 'Audience'). All but one of these women are Iranian; the exception is the French actress Juliette Binoche (who may or may not appear as herself), who nevertheless wears a veil.

In terms of the setting, this spectatorial experience is represented within what appears to be the interior of a contemporary movie theatre. We see seats in a space of near-darkness, as soft, flickering light (from behind, from an assumed projector that is never seen, and from the front, reflected off an

Figures 3.1–3.4 Some of the anonymous spectators shown in *Shirin*

assumed screen that is likewise never seen) illuminates the faces and features of the audience members.

Nevertheless, all is not as it appears. If the cinematic experience depicted in *Shirin* is faithful to a certain degree of realism, Kiarostami also subtly unravels this ontology. As the production process of *Shirin* reveals, what we think we see and hear is in fact the realisation of a complicated conceit or construction – a continuation, in this respect, of the modernism that characterises Kiarostami's earlier films. The seemingly straightforward premise of the film-within-the-film, and of our spectatorial act in watching an audience who in turn watch the film, is further complicated by a representational phantasmatic that challenges the ontological status of the movie theatre, audience and film-within-the-film, as represented.

First, the ostensible movie theatre constructed via the implied spatial relations between shots of women and their collective totality is a meticulously constructed illusion, which belies its seeming verisimilitude. As depicted in the making-of documentary *Taste of Shirin* (Hamideh Razavi, 2008), this theatre was created in Kiarostami's own living room. There are no rows of seats characteristic of a working movie theatre; there is no projection booth, projectionist or projector; rather, there are a handful of chairs illuminated by a simple lighting rig. 'Excuse me, is this a movie theatre?' asks one of the women in *Taste of Shirin*. The director's response outlines the contours of this meta-cinematic device:

> Yes, imagine it is a theatre. You have five minutes. During these five minutes, you are actually watching ninety minutes of the movie. [. . .] The more you forget that you are in front of the camera, and the more you think of yourself in a dark movie theatre, the better.

Kiarostami's direction is a necessary extension of this illusion since this is not an actual movie theatre with an audience, a collective grouping engaged in the simultaneous shared experience of watching a projected film in a public space. Beyond the small clusters of women in individual shots, the women who appear throughout the course of the film were never actually seated together at the same time and place, in a movie theatre or anywhere else. As Kiarostami's prompts reveal, these women are actors who now play the role of moviegoer.

In turn, in what is arguably *Shirin*'s most significant reflexive construction, the apparent film-within-the-film operates simultaneously as a more complex meta-cinematic device. This film, which we *believe* is watched, by what we *believe* is an audience of spectators in what we *believe* is a movie theatre, is not an extant work, but a fabrication. The spectatorial reactions of the represented women are responses neither to seeing nor hearing the story of Khosrow and Shirin, nor to any film at all. Rather, Kiarostami filmed these women as they acted the spectatorial role by simply imagining watching a film. It was only later that Kiarostami constructed – as a variation on the so-called Kuleshov effect – those auditory cues that prompt us to assume these women are watching and responding to a real film. Even then, this effect is not composed of images, but rather of a soundtrack alone. It is produced like a radio drama, which prompts us, according to James Naremore, 'to "see" a movie in our minds as we watch the play of emotion across women's faces and become conscious of our own role as cinematic spectators' (Naremore 2010: 21).

If the soundtrack of the film-within-the-film sutures and conceals the various elements that together constitute the reflexive conceit of *Shirin*, it also exists in a space of absence, forever beyond the frame of our own spectatorial experience, a ghost that haunts the periphery. In this respect, the sound is disembodied, separated from its apparent source, evoking Michel Chion's model of the voice without a body, or the '*acousmêtre*' (see, for example, Chion 1994 [1990], 1999 [1982]). Rooted in psychoanalytic understandings of a child's relationship with its mother, a disembodied voice suggests distance, separation and the absence of the mother's body, a 'dialectic of appearance and disappearance [that] is known to be dramatic for the child' (Chion 1999 [1982]: 17), according to Chion, and which can be transposed to the cinema.

In *Shirin*, in one such transposition of a dialectic of appearance and disappearance, a particular status is afforded the screen, whose negation, in conjunction with the film we hear without seeing, is most marked. The screen is inferred by the impression that a film is being projected and is the subject of an audience's gaze. Yet the screen is also conspicuous in its absence, its presence signified only in the light that flickers on the women's faces. By all appearances, we are witnessing the traditional cinematic experience associated with the movie theatre, but the fact that the screen itself is defined in spectral relief is symbolic, evocative of a certain lack – indeed, of death. If the cinema exists at all, *Shirin* suggests, it is in the form of a spectre.

For Negar Mottahedeh, the relative absence of women in Kiarostami's films prior to *Shirin* (and for which the principally female audience depicted in *Shirin* might be considered a conscious response) constitutes what amounts to an 'absent presence' (Mottahedeh 2008: 91), wherein 'the absent female body is associated with the enunciative apparatus, that is, with the very technology that produces his films' (Mottahedeh 2008: 100). The film-within-the-film of *Shirin* suggests a cinema itself on the cusp of presence and absence, and whose apparatus is enunciated only in a reflexive construction in which it is defined simultaneously in relief.

In short, the story of Khosrow and Shirin is the starting point for an elaborate phantasmatic that plays within an equally phantasmatic movie theatre, containing an apparent but ultimately negated screen and an audience of apparent but ultimately spectral spectators. This movie theatre – including apparatus, audience and film – is simultaneously present yet absent, real yet virtual, ontological yet hauntological. This is not the movie theatre as a realistic setting, but as a space of the cinematic imaginary. It is a psychogeographic or psychoarchitectural space, a projection of the authorial consciousness of Kiarostami with regard to the construction of cinema as a space of history and memory. At the same time, it also transcends the personal to engage with broader or collective conceptions of cultural memory, as the film opens up a reflexive space for exploring the changing ontology of cinema and the changing phenomenology of the cinematic experience.

Spectral Spectatorship

In constructing a virtual movie theatre, even as we are denied access both to a screen and to what we assume to be projected onto it, the focus of *Shirin* necessarily becomes those elements of the cinematic experience beyond a projected film. The illusion of temporal–spatial unity or coherence is exploited to reflexively explore a film historiography of time and place, evoking the theatrical exhibition more typical of an earlier era, with an emphasis on the site-specific cartographies of spectatorial affect. The meta-cinematic interrogates the cinematic, both in terms of what it means to be a member of a film audience, and the historical context that situates this experience as increasingly anachronistic, summoned as the spectre in a cinematic seance. Put another way, the hauntological becomes a means to explore the ontological, and vice versa, wherein the multiple valences of one complicate our understanding of the other.

Discourses on the cinematic experience have generally sought to account for the unique properties of the interaction of an individual, a film and the cinematic apparatus. This experience and its particular power necessarily changes over time. Ariel Rogers, for example, locates the 'cinematic experience in the interplay among the movie on the screen, the viewer confronting it, and the social and material configurations that inflect how this encounter is understood and felt' (Rogers 2013: 2), including those historically specific frameworks within which such encounters are experienced and might be understood. Similarly, Benson-Allott argues

> that the meaning-making process of watching a movie necessarily includes the mechanics of viewing, from the architecture of the theater to the location of the projector and the size of the screen, not to mention its constitutive components: the motion picture being screened and the human viewer. (Benson-Allott 2013: 3)

It is precisely these configurations and processes that *Shirin* explores in relation to the movie theatre, in historical context, and of which our own respective viewings of Kiarostami's film constitute reflexively abstracted parallels. This emphasis recalls Barthes's discussion of the distinctive psychic architecture of cinema, as experienced within the movie theatre. For Barthes, this space is one of 'hypnosis' (Barthes 1986 [1975]: 345), 'a veritable cinematographic cocoon' (Barthes 1986 [1975]: 346), in which the 'darkness of the cinema' (Barthes 1986 [1975]: 346) constitutes 'the very substance of reverie' (Barthes 1986 [1975]: 346).

In seeking to account for this reverie, Barthes identifies precisely those elements of the cinematic experience that surround the projected image itself – a notion of unique relevance to *Shirin* and its inferred but ultimately negated screen. For Barthes, the movie theatre comprises an 'image-repertoire' (Barthes 1986 [1975]: 348) that supersedes the images of any projected film, wherein '[t]he film image (including the sound) is what? A *lure*' (Barthes 1986 [1975]: 347). The recreation of the cinematic experience in *Shirin*, via its implied screen and film-within-the-film, forces us to resist such a lure. Instead, we encounter something closer to what Barthes describes as 'another way of going to the movies [. . .] by letting oneself be fascinated *twice over*, by the image and by its surroundings' (Barthes 1986 [1975]: 349). What is foregrounded are the very details of such surroundings, and the state of spectatorial hypnosis associated with the theatrical cinematic experience – even if *Shirin* articulates an era of existential uncertainty, as opposed to the more decidedly cinematic era in which Barthes was writing.

'How to forget that gaze, virtuous, tender and soft?' asks the eponymous protagonist of *Shirin*'s film-within-the-film. If Shirin speaks of a romantic lover whose absence is now mourned, she might equally be voicing, at a reflexive or meta-cinematic remove, a contemplative remembrance for the very act of cinematic spectatorship, which *Shirin* also explores. As Kiarostami notes of *Shirin*, such spectatorship is fundamental to his conception of cinema, and that a film does not exist until the audience sees it. As he contends, '[t]here is no such thing as a movie before the projector is switched on and after the theatre's lights are turned off. [. . .] In other words, at a certain juncture audiences and the movie become one' (cited in Khodaei 2009). Exploring that moment in which audiences and the movie become one, the succession of close-ups in *Shirin* emphasises the culture and practices of cinematic spectatorship, including the specific meanings and politics associated with the cinematic gaze.[6]

While it is beyond the purview of this particular discussion to explore these political implications in detail, it is worth noting that the explicitly gendered looking in *Shirin* nevertheless focuses our attention on the act of spectatorship, including the historical mode of cinematic experience contingent on the site of the movie theatre. For Hamid Naficy, connecting the gendered gaze within Iranian culture to a broader conception of cinematic spectatorship,

[n]ot only is the camera's gaze at each woman direct, close-up, and sustained for many seconds – violating the modesty rules – but also it captures its subjects in highly emotional and vulnerable states – by turn amused, delighted, touched, or weeping – resulting in a remarkably sensual and haptic spectatorial experience. (Naficy 2012: 134)

In terms of our viewing position, like the women who watch in their apparent movie theatre, we engage in a cognitive, sensory, psychological, emotional and physical interaction with the sounds and images before us – even if, in this instance, this affective experience is one step removed from a more directly experienced immersion in the fictional diegesis of a conventional narrative. Here, there is a consistent doubling of the cinematic experience as our own spectatorship mirrors what appears to be occurring on screen. In watching shot after shot of women who are themselves in the act of spectatorship, we necessarily become aware of our own role as spectators, including the specific conditions of exhibition – theirs as well as our own. Indeed, depending on the particular venue in which *Shirin* is experienced, we view spectators who appear to sit in the very same type of space as ourselves.

Irrespective of the exact site of our spectatorship, our spectatorial gaze meets and interacts with those of the women represented. Through this reflexive intertwining of audiences, the cinematic experience is heightened and reinforced as one that is not only an individual activity, but a communal, shared experience. In this doubled spectatorship, a dynamic of spectators and spectatorial proxies, *Shirin* constructs a mode of looking that Stephen Teo describes as 'inward space' (Teo 2013: 160–1), in which 'the subjective and the social are co-respondent and we are invited to take part, perhaps to share in their experience, but certainly to learn about all the affective and cognitive possibilities of the experience' (Teo 2013: 161).

This definition of cinematic spectatorship as one of shared experience has its roots in an imagined collectivity – the sense of community associated with the act of watching a film in a movie theatre as part of an audience, even if Kiarostami's underlying illusionism renders this space and its virtually connected moviegoers essentially spectral. For Asbjørn Grønstad, this representation of a collective spectatorial experience constitutes an 'aesthetics of ethical intimacy' (Grønstad 2012), by way of our negotiated relations with phantom proxies.

In this relationship, the span of our spectatorship emphasises the nature of cinema as a time-based medium, particularly with regard to the distinctive temporality associated with the movie theatre. In watching *Shirin*, we see the apparent film-within-the-film as experienced in real time, matching the duration of Kiarostami's film, which concludes only when the film-within-the-film itself concludes. For well over a century of projected cinema, and as Mulvey notes in her reference to 'a given narrative sequence', audiences have almost exclusively begun the viewing of a film at its beginning and ended at its end, a mode of spectatorship potentially at odds with the more directly or explicitly personalised consumption of other contemporary screen media and platforms.

More generally, in the film's representation of spectral bodies within the phantasmatic of the movie theatre, the very act of spectatorship exists in a dynamic relationship with film history and the changing sites and practices of film exhibition. The spectators in *Shirin* hover between presence and absence, embodiment and disembodiment, material and spectral. They represent an awareness of cinema and its history, precisely as the corpus of cinema, as a medium, is rendered ontologically uncertain through this reflexive rendering.

Again, the spectrality of this scenario is mirrored in the production process used to elicit the affective responses of those women who are filmed, and who summon the ghosts of their own memories of cinema, as conduits for our collective cultural memory. As documented in *Taste of Shirin*, rather than have actors gaze upon a projected film, Kiarostami instead had them return to their own experiences of cinema. On set, Kiarostami is heard directing: 'The movie is a type of movie you are relating to yourself inside and not out loud. [. . .] The movie has no director, no organiser. It is you and only you.' This affective prompt is an aide-memoire for each personal journey through prior cinematic experiences of the type *Shirin* now reconstructs as a reflexive phantasm. Each woman is represented not only in the cinematic present, but in a return to a cinematic past; they are filmed, despite appearances to the contrary, not in the act of watching a film, but in an act of remembrance, as memories of cinema return from the past and find new meaning in a reconfigured historical context.[7]

If *Shirin* explores the specificity of the cinematic experience, within the contours of the movie theatre as a site of gathering, it does so in relief, conjuring this space and its spectators as a complex phantasmatic. This site and this audience are subjected to a process of cinematic deconstruction, as they are placed within the context of a mode of representation that destabilises the very illusion and sense of presence that it constructs. This is an audience whose apparent collectivity conceals its more complex ontological status, as they inhabit a movie theatre whose own virtuality is likewise largely concealed. This symbolic experience is simultaneously constructed and deconstructed, placed within historical context as Kiarostami's late or post-cinematic lens reveals the implicit hauntology of this site and this act.

Allegorical Death and Hauntological Mourning

In exploring the hauntological resonances of projected cinema at a particular moment in film history, *Shirin* exists as an allegory for a broader conception of death, that of cinema itself, and functions as a form of 'mourning', in Derrida's terms, for that which is lost. Considered as a work of hauntology, through this act of mourning *Shirin* attempts to identify the remains of cinema, and to understand the nature of its spectre.

For Derrida, mourning is an essential element of hauntology that allows us to understand the origins or ontological source of a spectre, and the process of coming to terms with its loss. Addressing precisely what constitutes the '*thing*, spirit, or specter' (Derrida 1994 [1993]: 9) at the core of hauntology, Derrida responds that it is

> [f]irst of all, mourning. We will be speaking of nothing else. It consists always in attempting to ontologize remains, to make them present, in the first place by *identifying* the bodily remains and by *localizing* the dead [. . .] One has to know. *One has to know it. One has to have knowledge* [Il faut le savoir]. Now, to know is to know *who* and *where*, to know whose body it really is and what place it occupies – for it must stay in its place. In a safe place. (Derrida 1994 [1993]: 9)

To mourn is to know the body (that is, the corpse) and the place that it occupies in order to comprehend and contain a loss, a variation on Sigmund Freud's distinction between mourning (a necessary process for dealing with a lost love-object, whether literal or an abstraction) and melancholia (a pathologised internalisation of that process and a failure to detach from that which is lost) (Freud 1957 [1917]).

In Kiarostami's reflexively aware yet expressive mourning for cinema as a love-object, tears and the act of crying are given particular prominence as sonically signified via the apparent film-within-the-film and visually represented in the emotional responses of the women who appear to watch it. In terms of the latter, irrespective of the precise path to these affective responses – that is, whether in reaction to a film that is real or imagined – such tears (alongside other reactions and responses) nevertheless carry meaning, linking personal memory and collective cultural memory with regard to broader conceptions of cinema and the specific context of a mourning for its absence.

To some extent, the melodramatic fate of Khosrow and Shirin is also the fate of cinema. If tears are generically motivated in *Shirin*, a key element of the melodramatic and tragic forms to which its underlying tale belongs, they are also allegorical. In other words, one step removed, aligning melodramatic and meta-cinematic conceptions of loss and lamentation, it is also cinema that is mourned, and to the point of tears.

In the final minutes of *Shirin* in particular, the weeping of the audience members corresponds with the tearful climax of the film-within-the-film we assume they watch. As Shirin describes her own final moments, she addresses her female companions who are gathered before her in the fictional scenario or assumed diegesis of the film-within-the-film. Yet, she might equally be addressing the women who are gathered as the apparent audience in the apparent movie theatre that constitutes the representational dimension of *Shirin*. At a further remove, in terms of our own spectatorship, Shirin likewise addresses us as well, as an implied extension of these (meta-)cinematic collectives. On the soundtrack, we hear the denouement of her tale:

> You listen to my story and you cry. Through these tears, I see your eyes. Are you shedding these tears for me, Shirin? Or for the Shirin that hides in each one of you? Shirin who, through her life, received neither favour nor any attention. She was in love, a love that was never returned. She was lonely and no one believed her loneliness. Upon her death only, they would remember the young girl.

This narration, in which Shirin posthumously recounts her own death, is likewise a haunting of sorts. Moreover, in its explicit concern with death and remembrance, it evokes precisely those conceptions of mortality and memory that have marked recent discourses concerning cinema and its own supposed passing.

This reflexive layering of presence and absence, doubling and spectrality, is returned to during the closing credits of *Shirin*, as the eponymous protagonist reprises a lyric that Khosrow had earlier sung to her. Both voices are now joined in harmonic union, but only in death, and thus as a tragic lament:

> I am lost from within
> And from my own eyes
> I disappeared
> Like spindrift
> I melted in the sea
> I was a shadow
> At the beginning
> Lying down on the ground
> As soon as the sun
> Appeared
> I disappeared.

This ghostly duet of phantom lovers, like Kiarostami's own haunted conjuring of a cinema that has disappeared, is an evocation of light and shadow – those constituent elements of projected cinema – as well as the ephemeral presence of a shadow of reality that reminds us of cinema's own status as a kingdom of shadows.

In its allegorical doubling of death and the act of mourning, *Shirin* is an elegy of sorts. To identify and to know its lost object via a process of mourning, *Shirin* commemorates and memorialises, and thus preserves – in cinematically fossilised form – a passing mode of cinematic experience, and, by extension, the potential passing of cinema itself.

Defining the relationship between the ontological and the hauntological, between an object and its spectre, Derrida poses the following questions:

> *What is* a ghost? What is the *effectivity* or the *presence* of a specter, that is, of what seems to remain as ineffective, virtual, insubstantial as a simulacrum? Is there *there*, between the thing itself and its simulacrum, an opposition that holds up? Repetition *and* first time, but also repetition *and* last time, since the singularity of any *first time* makes of it also a *last time*. Each time it is the event itself, a first time is a last time. Altogether other. Staging for the end of history. Let us call it a *hauntology*. (Derrida 1994 [1993]: 10)

In the realm of cinema, *Shirin* exists as one such staging for the end of history, reflexively exploring the ontological and hauntological resonances of the medium, principally, as a site-specific experience.

In engaging the historical fate of cinema and of a particular cinematic experience, *Shirin* is an evocation (or invocation) of cinema as a haunted or spectral presence. The movie theatre and those within it are defined as much by absence as by presence. If this spectrality addresses the fundamentally illusory nature of cinema, and the ephemerality of the cinematic experience as it has existed throughout history, *Shirin* engages most specifically our contemporary historical consciousness of the medium, its apparatus and its sites of exhibition. It reminds us of the power of the projected moving image – as experienced collectively, in the darkened space of the movie theatre. This is an experience increasingly associated with the past, a remnant or relic of another era, whose contours are here cinematically mapped and memorialised. *Shirin* invites us to pay our respects to cinema and functions as an act of remembrance through which its spirit (or spectre) might live on.

Although it creates a decidedly reflexive phantasmatic, *Shirin* simultaneously resists a straightforward nostalgia, avoiding what Rashna Wadia Richards describes, for example, as the cinephilic pitfalls of 'mere obsession or fetishism or nostalgia' (Richards 2013: 217), in other words, a desire to simply recreate or return to the past. For Barber, 'the residual traces of film, notably those which appear to intimate its end, constitute vital materials for the instigation of new visual forms' (Barber 2010: 9), in an era in which cinema's 'apparent disintegration and obsolescence contrarily entail the originating of compulsive reinventions, with sensorial and ocular dimensions, of film and its spaces' (Barber 2010: 8). *Shirin* is one such compulsive reinvention, an attempt to identify and reframe our understanding of film and its spaces within a larger metaphorical or existential-historiographic context. Recognising the need to acknowledge the passing of a certain conception of cinema in order to create new forms, *Shirin* interrogates the very nature of cinema at a moment of ontological/hauntological transition. Neither a straightforward mourning, nor a nostalgic paean, there is a meta-fictional reflexivity in how it negotiates this historical context.

The movie theatre of *Shirin* can be read, in such terms, as a symbolic microcosm for a much wider cinematic context in terms of the film history embodied in this site and the erosion of its primacy. Derrida's figure of the spectre, and the broader concept of hauntology as revealed in *Shirin*, become models for understanding the nature of cinema more generally. If *Shirin*'s vision of cinema is fundamentally rooted in the unique experience of the movie theatre, it is, at this moment in history, archaic by design. For a fleeting moment of ontological/hauntological slippage, *Shirin* summons the theatrical cinematic experience once more – via those proxies who inhabit this particular movie theatre, on this particular day, in this particular location. Yet as a phantasmatic, the spectre evoked is also that of an entire moviegoing tradition and, arguably, an entire medium – all of the audiences who have ever attended a movie theatre, all of the movie theatres that have ever existed and all of the films that have ever played in them.

70×70: CINEMA AS MAPPED MEMORY

In a further memorial mapping, the focus of this chapter shifts to the city of London and to British novelist (and occasional filmmaker) Sinclair and his reflection on a lifetime of moviegoing in *70×70*, which constitutes a series of site-specific screenings and related documentation. In Sinclair's autobiographically, historically and geographically mapped account of cinematic spectatorship, specific encounters are historicised (the author's seventy years) and spatialised (the city of London). This temporal–spatial framing is further complicated by the historicity of autobiography and memories that continue to resonate – both individually, in terms of personal significance, and more broadly, in the wider sphere of a city-wide network of movie theatres, many of which no longer exist, as a symbol for cinema more generally. In its mapping of memory, *70×70* represents a further history of an absent present (or present absent), as if following any one of the spectral spectators of *Shirin* beyond the doors of Kiarostami's own movie theatre towards other sites and screenings, an entire lifetime of cinematic experiences, ultimately remembered and reimagined.

What connects *70×70* with *Shirin* is this shared emphasis on the sites of cinema, not least the movie theatre (in addition to the spectators and apparatus within and the lives and cities without), as mapped in the slippages of physical and psychic spaces, geographic and psychogeographic histories and individual cinematic experience and collective cultural memory. In each of these works, whether by way of Sinclair as the designated proxy of *70×70* or the audience of women in *Shirin*, the essence of cinema is framed as fleeting, ephemeral and in a complex dynamic with time, place and memory. In their pairing, we move from the psychoarchitectural space of the interior of the movie theatre to the further location and relocation of this symbolic site, mapped historically as situated in time and geographically as situated in space.

Where *70×70* diverges from *Shirin* is in shifting this reflexive concern from the filmic representation of a site of cinema in the meta-fictional *Shirin* to the programmed exhibition of such sites in the meta-curatorial *70×70*. Both *Shirin* and *70×70* recall cinema as an illusory spectacle, in movie theatres represented as sites of dialogue between past and present, spectatorship and its spectral shadow. Yet Sinclair is concerned with such mapping – of particular films, in particular movie theatres, each at its unique point in time and space – against the backdrop of a recognisably real location, London, as a microcosm for cinematic cities beyond. Accordingly, *70×70* addresses the fate of individual movie theatres as well as the cultures and practices of moviegoing more generally.

In this combination of histories spanning the individual and collective, material and immaterial, *70×70* is an illuminating act of experimental (and experiential) historiography, a useful model for how we might think about cinema today. In Sinclair's project, and in this chapter's analysis, occupying the literal and figurative spaces between ontology and hauntology, history and its haunting, such mapping exemplifies the contemporary status of cinema, located in geographic and psychogeographic sites and histories, of cinematic experiences and their mnemonic return.

Cinephilic Cartographies

Cinema is recalled in *70×70* as a site-specific experience, as Sinclair's historical encounters with cinema are located in personal history first, and then relocated in a series of contemporary screenings in creatively sited venues. Beyond nostalgia, this mnemonic network of cinematic experiences takes on new meaning in the present, both in terms of individual autobiography (in this instance, that of Sinclair and his remembrance) and the broader biography of the cinematic corpus (that is, film history). In this way, *70×70* connects individual and collective cultural memory; the realm of memoir, on the one hand, and the history (or histories) of an entire medium, on the other. The emphasis is on encounters that continue to exist in the present – even if in the form of memories now hazy, distant or dissociated of cultural practices now marginal, archaic or obsolete and of sites, venues and spaces that often no longer exist in cities which are themselves transformed beyond recognition.

On one level, *70×70* functions as a form of autobiography, the recollection and documentation of Sinclair's life, written on the occasion of his seventieth birthday. Yet, if this is a biography, it is also a cine-biography, a recurring dialogue with cinema, outlining as it does Sinclair's long-standing relationship with the medium. Sinclair recalls his own cinematic encounters – not only with films but also the specific contexts in which these films were experienced – which have shaped or otherwise represent his life. Seventy such films were selected, 'one for each year survived' (Sinclair 2014: 5).

In this framing of autobiography, which also functions as historiography, there is a certain conflation of self and cinema, in the form of the so-called cinephile – in this instance, Sinclair – who lives their life with and through the love of cinema. In such a conception, as with Sinclair, cinema might mark the contours of a human life and its cumulative experiences and memories.

At the same time, cinema is anthropomorphised as having both body and memory. Implicit in this notion is the idea that a mortal existence and the memories of this existence might also mark the historical bounds or contours of cinema, at least in metaphorical terms. Per such an abstraction, if *70×70* is an autobiography, memoir or life story of Sinclair, it might also represent a biography, memoir or life story of cinema, inscribed by way of Sinclair's own lived experiences and their explicit framing through memory and the broader span of the mortal-metaphorical life cycle.

In this meta-biographical or existential-historiographic schema, at the age of seventy (in the instance of Sinclair), and many decades older (in the instance of cinema), the cumulative memory of this life (for Sinclair, literal; for cinema, metaphorical) weighs heavily, perhaps to the point of implied finitude or mortality. Putting to one side the possible end point of such a span, what is also of note in this dual analogy (life lived as cinema, cinema as life lived) are the revealing parallels and interactions of human memory and film history through which we might recount these respective histories.

As Annette Kuhn *et al.* remind us, discussing film history in terms of the cinematic experience and our recollections of these experiences, 'cinema memory – people's memories of the essentially social activity of going to the cinema – can form part of a broader stream of cultural or collective memory' (Kuhn *et al.* 2017: 5). In Sinclair's cinema memory, as one such mediation of individual and collective significance, specific memories engage this broader stream in a number of illuminating ways.

Looking back, in Sinclair's life-defining selections of films and experiences there is no claim of universality, nor even the clarity of historical certainty. Rather, as qualification, or '[b]y way of explanation', as Sinclair puts it, the aim was

> [t]o make my choices function more like a novel of mysterious disconnected fragments. Read or view in any order. The 70 entries compose a botched portrait of author-as-viewer. Many hours of the life under consideration had been spent talking on the telephone about films. Talking

in cars about films, while driving to the next cinema. Dreaming films. Walking films. And occasionally, very occasionally, actually making one. (Sinclair 2014: 5)

In the intersections of personal biography and collective memory, Sinclair's talking, driving, dreaming and walking offer routes towards the broader history of life under consideration of cinema itself.

The resulting list is deliberately eclectic, consciously eschewing any attempt at objectivity or canonicity. Rather, as one might expect of any individual, Sinclair's cinematic encounters are idiosyncratic, illustrating a personal journey through what Alain Bergala describes as 'the continent of cinema' (Bergala 2016 [2006]: 13), referring to the terrain of cinematic experience. As Bergala explains,

[a]ll of those for whom cinema has been important in life, not as a simple pastime but as an essential element of their constitution, and who knew very early on that they would dedicate their lives, in one way or another, to this art – these individuals all hold in their heads an imaginary auto-biography, a cinematic version of their life. (Bergala 2016 [2006]: 12)

In the instance of Sinclair, as one example of an individual for whom cinema has been central to their existence, this imaginary autobiography is imaginary no longer, but is written and further enacted or re-enacted in *70×70* and its contemporary screenings.

These selections, each of which marks a moment in his life, include Sinclair's own films – such as *Swandown* (2012), which he wrote with director Andrew Kötting – but also an eclectic mix of Hollywood studio films, B-pictures and curios, art cinema, cult and experimental films, documentaries and others.

Notably, in seeking 'to sift the residue of autobiography' (Sinclair 2014: 5), this personal history is also rooted in the histories of specific sites, situating film history within the interconnections of cultural memory and physical geography. For example, Sinclair writes of Jean-Luc Godard's *Le Mépris* (1963), 'I remember seeing this one at the National Film Theatre on the night I left London for the Mediterranean island of Gozo' (Sinclair 2014: 16). He describes Orson Welles's *A Touch of Evil* (1958) as '[a] film that has been a point of reference since I saw it on its original release (as a second feature) at the Paris Pullman' (Sinclair 2014: 31). Elsewhere, Sinclair recalls Joseph Losey's *The Criminal* (1960) as

[t]he reason for my first excursion to Dalston. I was a film student in Brixton, on the other side of the river, and came across, getting the bus from Liverpool Street for the first of many rides in the direction of the Rio [Cinema]. (Sinclair 2014: 39)

In *Cartographic Cinema* (Conley 2007), Tom Conley outlines cinema's long history of visualising or representing the map, and in the instance of Sinclair this process is reversed, with cinema itself mapped in time and space as geo-located memoir.

Sinclair's own history, he suggests, is defined by the films that have shaped him, but also by the sites and contexts of each cinematic encounter, including the relationship of these experiences to the broader history of a changing medium. From biography to historiography, cinemascape to cityscape, Sinclair's cinephilic cartographies would be further recounted and recalled in the present, charted in the contemporary resonances of historical films, sites and geographies.

Remapping the Memory of Cinema

Having initially selected a series of films, a further curatorial or historio-graphic act saw the organisation of these films into site-specific screenings in newly mapped (that is, remapped) locations. In this way, these films and their significance are relocated and now experienced in altogether different historical contexts, both in the life of the author and the history of cinema. Sinclair's mapping is thus twofold: in the first instance, the original context (film, screening, site, city, biography) in which each film was first encountered; in the second instance, the precise location for each newly curated screening, across a network of plotted pathways both geographic and mnemonic, to our understanding of film history.

Across the course of a year, from July 2013 to June 2014, Sinclair's seventy films were presented in site-specific screenings – approximately fifty in total, including a number of double bills, collections of shorts and other curatorial combinations – and subsequently catalogued in a book that maps and other-wise documents these screenings.

In their specific settings, these chosen venues constitute a further variable or vector in terms of historicity. Each film finds new context in its biographical, historical and geographical relocation. Significance resides in the continuing interplay of physical site and mnemonic resonance, the transformations of place and the transformations of memory, not only in the act of remembrance but in the new settings in which these memories find meaning.

Notably, these settings include not only traditional or official sites of cinema, but sites and spaces far beyond the recognised movie theatre. This is acknowledgement, perhaps, of the gradual disappearance of the specific venues that Sinclair recalls, of a wider displacement of movie theatres, but also an embrace of potential routes to revised engagement with this history, seeking out the unexpected and undiscovered. If the venues of *70x70* include a num-ber of familiar institutions of cinema and arts exhibition – including London's

Barbican Centre, Institute of Contemporary Arts and Whitechapel Gallery, for example – Sinclair's principal concern is with situating the memory of cinema in less typical sites. As he describes it, this project was not intended to be 'another strategic menu compiled for film buffs, but a year-long curation on boats, in shop windows, parks and palaces' (Sinclair 2014: 5), with the intention of exploring the psychic reverberations of these settings in a dynamic with the recollection of film history as a site-specific experience.

What follows are just a few illustrative examples: *The Dark Eyes of London* (Walter Summers, 1939), a horror film set in London, was screened in the gothic surrounds of the long-defunct Wapping Hydraulic Power Station, built on the banks of the River Thames in the 1890s; Fritz Lang's *Dr. Mabuse* series (1922–1960),[8] whose titular criminal mastermind is a medium who specialises in hypnosis, telepathy and bodily possession, was screened in Swedenborg Hall of the Swedenborg Society, an organisation devoted to the legacy of eighteenth-century spiritualist Emanuel Swedenborg; while John Smith's *The Girl Chewing Gum* (1976) – a work filmed in East London – was screened at the now-closed The White Building arts venue, just east of the Kingsland Road (and Odeon movie theatre) it depicts, albeit in a radically different cinematic as well as urban geography.

Despite superficial similarities, these screenings are very different from – and, arguably, a conscious reaction against – the so-called event cinema trend of recent years and its apparent attempt to commercially differentiate projected cinema as exhibited in non-traditional spaces and themed configurations, whether on rooftops, in mobile movie theatres or other unusual settings. After all, in Sinclair's staging of the cinematic experience, the underlying event in question – namely Sinclair's initial spectatorship – occurred many years or even decades prior in terms of an original ontology, only now to return as remembrance and re-enactment, at one step removed from the primary lived (that is, cinematic) experience it recalls.

To consider one of these screenings in greater detail, we might return to the Wapping Hydraulic Power Station (which, at the time of Sinclair's screening, housed The Wapping Project arts venue) and *The Dark Eyes of London*. In terms of plot, Sinclair describes the story of 'a maniac who runs a Thamesside home for the blind' (Sinclair 2014: 45), which serves as a counterpoint to a building now vested, if for one night only, with the vision of cinema and the sight and gaze of cinematic spectatorship. In Sinclair's introduction to the screening (on 27 July 2013), he further describes the unique intersections of place, biography, memory and film:

> I've been connected with this place for a long time. [. . .] A suitable backdrop to this adventure with English gothic, *The Dark Eyes of London*, derived from Edgar Wallace.

The reason I'm here is because of the special quality of exactly where we find ourselves, in relation to the river, and in relation to all the forms of life that emerge from the river. Coming here, every time is a renewal. You look down on the mud, the tide is low. [. . .] What a great title to consider, *The Dark Eyes of London*, it tells you everything . . . (Sinclair 2014: 63)

On the banks of the Thames and in a building whose original occupation and occupants have long since been replaced, Sinclair elicits the transience of memory (his own and that of a broader cinematic archive of films, sites and experiences) and of place. Moreover, he does so in a venue that is itself now a symbol of transient vitality – the dynamism of generated power, most obviously, but also the life of cinema – and, more latterly, a transient cultural geography.[9]

Another example is the screening of Lang's *Dr. Mabuse* films at the Swedenborg Society (on 30 July 2013), replete with its legacy of spiritualism and the mediation between living and dead. The sense of ontological uncanniness at the core of the original films, especially in the shape of the disembodied Dr. Mabuse, is amplified when situated in the modern home of Swedenborg's spiritualist legacy and symbolises cinema as spirit (or, in Derrida's terms, spectre). Sinclair describes the *Dr. Mabuse* films as 'haunting' (Sinclair 2014: 12), adding further that their titular 'super-criminal, coiner, demagogue, stagey actor, voice behind the curtain in an empty room, is the defining presence (absence) of the new metropolis' (Sinclair 2014: 13). As Sinclair explains in his introduction to the screening, 'I couldn't imagine a better setting for the *Mabuse* films. [. . .] Here is the cusp between science and magic, between the technology of cinema and the ancient ritualistic behaviour of a city' (Sinclair 2014: 64). Considered in relation to cinema, including its technology or apparatus as configured at the site of projection, such a gathering is an embodied summoning of disembodied spirits (returning memories, passing patrons, representational conjurings and the fundamental magic of the cinematic apparatus as projected illusion and reanimation). Moreover, it is a recognition of the increasingly fleeting and even deathly nature of cinema and its sites, apparatus and associated spectatorship.

Elsewhere, Sinclair's screening of *The Girl Chewing Gum* (on 22 October 2013) represents a further instance of a film history whose past continues to haunt the present. Originally filmed in East London, *The Girl Chewing Gum* was also screened there in its *70×70* curation, though not at the movie theatre (the Odeon Dalston) so prominently depicted in the film, for that has long since disappeared,[10] outlived by the memorial record of the film itself, but also by Sinclair's memories of the film and of first seeing and hearing it. This is a film defined by place, but it is a sense of place – and, in some respects, cinema – that has been transformed. As Sinclair writes, '[t]he John Smith film, locked to its significant corner, alongside a now vanished cinema, is a classic of place. This place: a tributary of Kingsland Road within hawking distance of Dalston Junction. All human life was there' (Sinclair 2014: 46). This past tense 'was', as opposed to a present tense 'is', reminds us that the cinematic London of today is not the same as in prior decades – even if this past remains palpable in the present in altered form.

This point is made by Smith himself in his 2011 reworking, *The Man Phoning Mum*, also screened by Sinclair (on the same evening in the same venue as *The Girl Chewing Gum*). This later film revisits the original London location of *The Girl Chewing Gum* thirty-five years later. As well as rhyming titles (from 'Gum' to 'Mum') and the connections of gendered protagonists ('Girl' and 'Man') in the midst of a verb ('Chewing' and 'Phoning') that suggest connections across periods and works, this sequel of sorts meticulously retraces the same camera movements as the original film. The result is a near-facsimile photographic representation in spatial terms, but an articulation that is displaced by decades, in temporal terms. The contemporary footage – colour, shot on video in 2011 – is superimposed over the original film – black-and-white, shot on celluloid in 1976 – the underlying footage from which fades in and out over the course of the composite film's approximately twelve minutes, during which the audio from the original film is heard in full.

At the point at which *The Man Phoning Mum* depicts the movie theatre of *The Girl Chewing Gum*, it is necessarily via the underlying 1976 footage of the earlier film, as now reprised but also obscured by the superimposed image of the same location as filmed in 2011, where an apartment block now sits on the site of the former movie theatre. A metal fence surrounds the apartments and appears to enclose, via graphical and historical superimposition, the movie theatre of 1976 and its line of queueing patrons, who are suspended forevermore as they wait to enter a movie theatre that no longer exists. When, on the soundtrack, the original 1976 voiceover narrator directs, '[i]n the cinema queue, I want to see a boy and his mother . . .', we see no such cinema or queue, but instead the brick exterior of the apartments that now stand in its place. The original soundtrack is split off from its corresponding image track as film history itself is transposed into the present as a reminder and signifier of that which is absent. 'The new interrogation, from the same position, is a well-judged conceit', notes Sinclair in his introduction to the screening. 'Past and present dig elbows. Dalston is honoured' (Sinclair 2014: 46). Form meets content in both Smith's film and Sinclair's screening, each of which functions as a visual and mnemonic trace of a now absent past – of a place, of a movie theatre and of a broader culture of moviegoing – in Smith's formal realisation and Sinclair's curatorial refrain.

Figure 3.5 *The Man Phoning Mum*, one of the films documented in *70×70: Unlicensed Preaching: A Life Unpacked in 70 Films*

Here and elsewhere, past and present dig elbows in each of Sinclair's approximately fifty contemporary screenings of seventy historical films, in sites and contexts ripe with memory and meaning, which find new associations in altered settings. The memory of cinema is recalled and relocated as Sinclair navigates and negotiates the evolving history of this medium and the historicity of its sites and spectatorship.

The Cinematic Experience and Its Trace

What is especially notable about the screenings of *70×70* is the extent to which they are deliberately historically and ontologically unrooted. Put simply, these films and Sinclair's memories of them are recalled in very different conditions, against the interconnected backdrops of urban change on the one hand, and the relocation of the cinematic experience on the other. The movie theatre, in this configuration, functions as a locus of memory, a psychogeographic conception extended still further in Sinclair's material mapping of immaterial traces.

In certain respects, Sinclair's acts of remembrance echo Cavell's discussion of the cinematic experience and the abstraction of mnemonic recollection, even if now recontextualised in significant ways. Foreshadowing Sinclair by almost fifty years, Cavell writes of his own encounters as private knowledge, unique to an individual. Reflecting on 'the experiences of films that I have cared about' (Cavell 1971: 9), Cavell outlines a distinctive phenomenology of projected cinema – of being part of an audience, at a distinct time and place, at a particular moment in one's life. This distinctiveness is bound up in a sense of temporal specificity, including the never-to-be-repeated conditions of a single screening/viewing, an ontology whose abstraction exists in the form of memories that might return as the evocation of an original experience.

Identifying the ephemerality of the cinematic experience as a way of highlighting the ontological primacy of the original encounter, Cavell sets the stage for our later concern with the interconnectedness of ontological and hauntological states, an object or experience and its virtuality or spectre. Cavell recounts his own encounters with cinema as

> hours and days of awe; momentous, but only for the moment; unrecapturable fully except in memory and evocation; gone. If you see them now for the first time, you may be interested and moved, but you can't know what I know. (Cavell 1971: 10)

These city-specific, site-specific, historically specific experiences are never universally shared among a group, even when gathered within the same site, on the same day, for the same screening of the same film. Rather, the cinematic experience is framed as uniquely personal – rooted in biography, in the moment, and in the contingencies of mnemonic recollection, a retrospective.

This is the type of gathering that Sinclair recalls – and evokes (or recaptures, in Cavell's term) in its contemporary re-enactment – an affective encounter, except now it is the reflection of a reflection. We are viewing a world within a world, to reference Cavell's own notions of 'the world viewed' (Cavell 1971) and his 'reflections on the ontology of film' (Cavell 1971). If, via *70×70*, Sinclair does indeed invite us to know what he knows, it is with full awareness that to do so now is to experience and thus know something else entirely, a reflection not on the ontology of film in other words, but on the hauntology of film. In Sinclair's contemporary curation, the memory of the experience assumes primacy over the experience itself and returns as its own type of haunting.

If Cavell's concern with the cinematic experience engages the personal memory of an individual experience within a collective act, what has changed since the period in which Cavell was writing is the extent to which the culture, sites and apparatus of projected cinema have also been consigned to a figurative space of history and memory, amidst a more literal erasure of the physical sites (and the spectatorship therein) of that cinema.

In fact, Sinclair's contemporary mapping actively engages the fundamental impermanence of architectures and geographies, including the specific sites of cinema, as one manifestation of the type of abandonment articulated by Barber, among others, but also as a route to the resonant realm of memory and evocation described by Cavell, in lieu of an underlying ontology.

In Barber's case, it is the cinematic city of Los Angeles, not London, that is the explicit focus of a metropolitan mapping of what might also represent a broader phenomenon beyond any one specific city.[11] Barber details how, over time, the movie theatres of Los Angeles have been bulldozed, left to crumble and otherwise repurposed in a way broadly analogous to a larger decline in cinema, especially its projected forms. Charting his own cultural geography, rooted in film history, Barber argues that

[o]nce the end of film has been located, the eye can travel in any direction, backwards in time, forwards in time, or more profoundly into a moment of immediacy, and into the transformative space and corporeality of filmic ruination. Film's end is a matter for the human eye, for memory, and oblivion. (Barber 2010: 11)

Such mapping locates the movie theatre in particular as an ontologically uncertain or ambiguous site, a nexus of memory that transposes the time and space of history and geography.

Transplanted to London, with the simultaneous backwards in time and forwards in time at the core of Sinclair's own explorations of film history in each of his cinematic stagings, the past is reconfigured in the present through the active negotiation of such sites of eye, memory and oblivion – of movie theatres and cities as they experience the effects of physical and mnemonic decay.

The status of projected cinema reflects – and, in some instances, directly reveals – the physical and cultural geographies of a city in flux (London, in the instance of Sinclair). These spaces, too, have undergone considerable change, and open up cracks for the historiographer to summon the past into the present as an intervention into these spaces and their everyday functions. In this dynamic, if the city offers a means to navigate the history of cinema, this history offers a means of navigating the city and its transformations anew, both as the mediated exploration of space and the spatialised exploration of media – in this instance, the medium of cinema.

In this regard, *70x70* has clear links to the theories and practices of psychogeography. As the term implies, psychogeography exists in the compound relationship between psychology and geography, in terms of how space and place interact with subjective experience, and vice versa. For Guy Debord, most famously, psychogeography – as differentiated and opposed to geography – comprises 'the study of the precise laws and specific effects of the geographical environment, consciously organized or not, on the emotions and behavior of individuals' (Debord 1981 [1955]: 5). These concerns are visualised, for example, in his *Guide psychogéographique de Paris: Discours sur les passions de l'amour* (Debord 1957), a map of the city that depicts, in the translation of its subtitle, not the more typical terrain of empirical geographies, but the enigmatic or esoteric mapping of a 'discourse on the passions of love', reimagining Paris in terms of the affairs of the heart. To the extent that Debord was concerned with urban spaces, it was not in the service of urban planning in any conventional sense of the term, rather as a route to less tangible elements and forces.

Applied to Sinclair's own distinctive cartography – of London as a city of cinematic experience – *70×70* might also be thought of as an act of psychogeography; perhaps, even, as a discourse on the passions of love. Such passions might extend, in the instance of Sinclair, to the particular love of the cinephile and their mappings, and such a notion might also encompass the possibility of love lost as well as found, both the experience and its remembrance. Clearly, Sinclair's concern is far from a conventional mapping of the movie theatres of London, nor those of any specific city – for which one might turn to other maps and measures – but rather the mutual interactions of the city and the emotions and behaviour of individuals, both in the instance of Sinclair, as one such individual or proxy, and the plural of our collective spectatorship, that is, of moviegoing more generally.

For Debord – and in certain respects, for Sinclair – there would be a political dimension to this subversion of geographically ordered existence. In the 1950s in Paris, psychogeography was conceived as a challenge to existing geographies and a certain logic in city planning and architectural design. In the contemporary moment in London, to reinterpret geographies and imagine alternatives, traversing cultural paths and documenting the sites of cinema in the instance of marking their absence, is to also highlight the contested dimensions of a city of urban development and shifting demographics that displace as well as place, demolish as well as build and evict as well as house. The staging of a remembered cinematic past in the very context of a passing cinematic present, in Sinclair's mappings of place and memory (or memory and place), is both an historiographic and political act, one of shared cultural spaces and individual navigations as well as shared cultural memory and the constituent mnemonics of individual experience and recollection.

The intention – whether of Debord in the mid-1950s or Sinclair in the present – is not simply to record, but to reinterpret and redefine; to suggest alternative routes and ways of navigating existing geographies and their histories. In Sinclair's playful and provocative sitings of cinema, whether in the instance of *The Dark Eyes of London* in a disused power station, the *Dr. Mabuse* films in the home of a spiritualist, *The Girl Chewing Gum* in the streets of East London or any other of the approximately fifty screenings of seventy films, *70×70* provides a map, too, for how we might navigate the present, whether by way of geographical mappings of space or historiographic mappings of time, charting and creating new histories and memories in the process.

Ultimately, at the spatialised intersections of individual and collective memory, *70×70* maps and remaps cinema to recall its past (or pasts) into new spaces for engaging film history. Sinclair reminds us not only of the importance of the movie theatre as a site of lived experience, but also of the immaterial resonances of these material sites and practices. *70×70* is explicitly concerned with the past, not a nostalgic return, but rather an engagement with the irrevocability of the past as it continues to exist in the present. It appears in relief as a reminder of certain absences – of physical sites, of personal moments (for Sinclair, seventy times over) and of a shared cultural heritage – as the memory of one particular life lived through cinema is recollected and revisited as a cinematic and mnemonic trace.

CONCLUSION

Catherine Fowler asks '[h]ow do we look back to cinema's past without feeling its loss? How do we recall cinema's past without proclaiming its end?' (Fowler 2012: 28). As Kiarostami and Sinclair remind us in their dovetailing reflections on the sites and experiences of cinema, to look back and acknowledge a sense of loss is not necessarily to succumb to an inevitable conception of finitude, a crippling nostalgia or overwhelming mourning. In the reflexive contours of spectatorship (as well as re-enactment) of *Shirin* and the mapping (as well as remapping) of *70×70*, there is a conscious awareness of the need to interrogate the processes of memory and mourning.

The movie theatre in particular, so richly imbued with historical memory, offers an especially resonant symbolic locus for this redefinition of cinema – in this instance, by way of examining space as historiographic acts. As the sites and practices of cinema's past are reconfigured in the present – in altered ontological state – the meanings and significations of these sites require a history that is cognisant of this hauntology, as past and present continue to coexist in a period of slippage or transition.

In a context in which the hauntological becomes a fitting theoretical and historical model for understanding cinema, the need for a refined historiography is compelling. The metaphor of a media archaeology that sifts through the sediment of the past is, in the case of the movie theatre, rendered more precise in relation to the substrate of movie theatres shuttered, levelled or razed and the physical, psychic and other consequences of these acts. Both *Shirin* and *70×70* suggest a sense of history conversant with the nature of memory and the very fragility, fallibility and ephemerality of cinema itself, including in the form of theatrical projection and in the sprawling networks of public sites that historically housed it.

What might we glean from Kiarostami's and Sinclair's respective rout-ings of film history via personal memoir – real or illusory, remembered or re-enacted – and as spatially mapped? In these instances of spatialised media archaeology and the memorial mapping of space, place and trace via the movie theatre, we move towards a psychohistoriography of sorts. Here, the spectre of cinema is both recognised and revealed, suggesting that a nuanced understanding engages the past precisely as it haunts the present. Such a history maps shifting architectures and geographies, but also, as Kiarostami and Sinclair so usefully chart in their cinematic cartographies, the spectres that reside within them.

Recalling the Past Lives of Cinema: *Uncle Boonmee Who Can Recall His Past Lives*

Chapter 3 focused on the site of the movie theatre and its particular apparatus and associated cinematic experience. To develop the idea further, this chapter considers more closely one specific element of the evolving cinematic apparatus: photochemical film or its absence. The material base of celluloid of one format or gauge or another has been replaced by digital formats to the point at which this transition is now effectively complete. As a result, film has assumed a niche or specialist status, restricted to gallery practice, for example, or specific use as a pastiche or other marker of film historical practices and periods.

In this contemporary historical and cultural context in which the memory, uses or other evocation of film persist, a degree of ontological and historical ambiguity has arisen, a symbolic vestige that continues to find resonance and meaning, even in – or perhaps because of – an increasingly immaterial cinematic present. The historicity and signifiers associated with this medium have come to represent the past, a materiality out of place, replete with associations of finitude, obsolescence and even death.

With regard to how we might progressively historicise these shifts, and in the process, complicate proclamations of demise and the sense of loss that has accompanied the erosion of the primacy of film, we should consider not just the significance of this shift with regard to material practices (noting an absence), but also the more intangible expressions of a contemporary material–immaterial slippage.

In fact, in terms of the wider lens of a macro-historical perspective, moments of rupture are implicit in an existential historiography in which cycles of change are considered essential and recurrent, rather than an existential threat that is absolute, to be resisted or otherwise lamented. Technological change, such as the film-to-digital transition of recent years, is often greeted with just such a reactionary response.

It is precisely this notion of meta- or macro-historical cycles, of inevitable and necessary transition and transformation, that comes to the fore in Apichatpong Weerasethakul's *Uncle Boonmee Who Can Recall His Past Lives* (*Loong Boonmee raleuk chat*, 2010), which is presented here as one particular case study in the persistence of photochemical film, even if in the form of a phantasm.

UNCLE BOONMEE WHO CAN RECALL HIS PAST LIVES: THE PHANTASM OF PHOTOCHEMICAL FILM

Filmed on Super 16mm at a time of the increasing obsolescence of photochemical film as a medium, *Uncle Boonmee Who Can Recall His Past Lives* can be analysed not only as a reflection on the death and dying of its protagonist and his memories of past lives, but also in terms of how we might understand cinema and its evolving film-to-digital material base. In this broader context, the film's representation of reincarnation – a cycle of birth, death and rebirth across a range of enigmatically embodied entities – has much to say about the history of cinema and its own path through multiple incarnations.

In foregrounding the corporeality of Uncle Boonmee's physical form at the precise moment of his passing, and as framed in the context of the material–immaterial slippages of his returning past lives and the film's other ghostly or ontologically uncertain presences, *Uncle Boonmee Who Can Recall His Past Lives* also engages the materiality of cinema itself. The physical medium of photochemical film, in particular, carries parallel resonances in terms of its capacity to preserve time, memorialising lives whose return from the past might constitute a haunting of sorts, not unlike the revenant return of Uncle Boonmee's past lives.

In recent years, photochemical film has faced its own death, as this medium has been increasingly replaced by digital formats. The use of film has assumed its own ghostly resonance, manifesting a materiality whose visual qualities have become increasingly associated with the past, and which now carry a series of potent signifiers of memory, materiality, mutability and mortality. Its use as a representational strategy is thus a corollary of the central themes of *Uncle Boonmee Who Can Recall His Past Lives* as well as a means of reflexively framing a broader historiographic exploration of the nature of cinema in the context of its evolving film-to-digital base and its own historical cycle of birth, death and beyond.

Expanding the fictional scenario of *Uncle Boonmee Who Can Recall His Past Lives*, notions of transmigration and reincarnation exist as useful existential-historiographic metaphors for understanding and conceptualising an expanded history of cinema. Nuancing the discussion of cinema's own potential death, they both challenge and offer alternatives to the precisely delineated demise and singular conception of finitude that mark much of the prevailing discourses concerning the status of cinema today.

In short, like the animal and other forms that Uncle Boonmee has assumed in past lives, will the soul or spirit of cinema live on, beyond death, transcending the corporeality of a single, dying body through an equivalent process of transmigration or reincarnation?

Metaphors of Birth and Death

Uncle Boonmee Who Can Recall His Past Lives is revealing in the context of debates concerning the supposed death of cinema and what we might describe as an existential historiography or metaphorical life cycle of birth and death. These debates are part of what André Gaudreault and Philippe Marion suggest is 'a recurring theme in film history' (Gaudreault and Marion 2015 [2013]: 26), in terms of discourses concerning what they describe as 'the process of dying' (Gaudreault and Marion 2015 [2013]: 13). In 1953, André Bazin posed the very question '[i]s cinema mortal?' and responded thus: 'The fact that one can reasonably ask oneself such a question today, and that it requires some thinking through to come to an optimistic answer, should be enough to justify astonishment and musing' (Bazin 2014 [1953]: 313).[1] Beyond the today of Bazin's 1953, for Gaudreault and Marion, such discourses are most marked in those 'periods whose technological innovations are of such intensity that they call into question cinema's identity as a medium' (Gaudreault and Marion 2015 [2013]: ix).

Engaging a contemporary period of such intensity, and exploring the formal and other properties that arise out of a historically specific conception of cinema's theorised mortality, *Uncle Boonmee Who Can Recall His Past Lives* suggests the alternative models of transmigration and reincarnation. These models arrive via the titular lives of Uncle Boonmee, abstracted in metaphorical relief as ways of understanding the potential incarnations of cinema as well as its cycle of life. In its schema of existential transformations and embodiments, of fluid boundaries across human, animal and other forms, *Uncle Boonmee Who Can Recall His Past Lives* explores cinema's own existential status, with a particular focus on the materiality of photochemical film as a corporeal embodiment, framed according to an existential historiography that equates the increasing obsolescence of film to a death of sorts.

In certain respects, the meanings associated with the cinematic representation of death are necessarily specific to the medium of representation and its own set of signifiers. As Michele Aaron argues, '[d]eath, which is repressed or inaccessible in real life, returns in culture in various forms, genres and guises' (Aaron 2014: 12) that include 'the specificities of the technology or media that manage this return' (Aaron 2014: 12) and which represent the possibility 'to do death differently' (Aaron 2014: 12). Put another way, when it comes to death, not all moving image media are equal. Part of the potential to do death differently, in the instance of *Uncle Boonmee Who Can Recall His Past Lives*, is a reflexive engagement with the mortality of cinema itself and the specificities of the technology or media that structure these representations.

Most explicitly, in *Uncle Boonmee Who Can Recall His Past Lives*, the historiographic narrative of cinema's own supposed mortality is reflected in a fictional scenario that foregrounds themes of death and dying and a life cycle that encompasses the possibility of transmigration or reincarnation. In his final days, suffering from kidney failure, Uncle Boonmee recalls his past lives. Human, animal and other non-human forms are depicted, as we witness what we assume to be his prior incarnations and a soul or spirit that migrates from one body to the next, across species and spanning natural and supernatural forms. This journey towards death – and implied transformation – is one that sees Uncle Boonmee reflect on the nature of mortality and the relationship between body and soul.

In broadly allegorical terms, the failing physical form of Uncle Boonmee references the changing materialities of cinema in this narrative of mortality. In short, as Uncle Boonmee prepares to end one life and begin another, materially embodied or otherwise, the story of his transmogrification or reincarnation, and his succession of lives, is also that of cinema.

In more precisely metaphorical terms, the very conscious decision to shoot *Uncle Boonmee Who Can Recall His Past Lives* on film (Super 16mm subsequently transferred or blown up to 35mm for theatrical distribution) at a time when more and more films are shot and exhibited on digital formats likewise engages conceptions of the cinematic apparatus as a body of sorts, including the particular embodiment of photochemical film, and a soul that moves through multiple incarnations.

For Apichatpong, there is an alternative to death as a singular moment of finitude – both for Uncle Boonmee, within the fiction, and for cinema, beyond the fiction. In this expanded existential framework, the emphasis is on the passing of the soul into an altogether different or unexpected form upon death.

In fact, *Uncle Boonmee Who Can Recall His Past Lives* is based on a sermon book by a Buddhist monk,[2] and while the film's concerns with life after death are also secular, the broader context of a Buddhist theology or philosophy is central to its narrative of death and reincarnation. Ronald Green describes the film as 'in line with basic Buddhist analysis of perception' (Green 2014: 131–2), but also a questioning of 'Buddhism as a conservative force' (Green 2014: 131).

This reading resists what David Teh regards as a tendency towards discussing Apichatpong's films in terms of 'mystification and exoticism' (Teh 2011: 595), instead placing Apichatpong as auteur and *Uncle Boonmee Who Can Recall His Past Lives* as text within transnational circuits of film production, distribution and culture. Considered in these contexts, the director's decision to shoot on film means that the work engages but also transcends regional, national and religious concerns to also address the lives of film as a conversation conducted in global cinema.

In the context of materialities that are literal as well as metaphorical, particular meaning is located in the passing of the soul into animal form, including animist-influenced ideas of animal-to-human and human-to-animal transmigration or reincarnation, and of a more general conception of animism. With regard to this fluidity, May Adadol Ingawanij explains animism and its links to cinema in terms of 'the permeability of human and nonhuman worlds' (Ingawanij 2013: 91) and a sense of history 'characterised by untimely appearances and the cyclical trajectory of rebirths and returns' (Ingawanij 2013: 91). These features describe precisely the media-metaphorical narrative of *Uncle Boonmee Who Can Recall His Past Lives*, as rooted in the culture of the Isan territory of north-east Thailand.[3]

Uncle Boonmee Who Can Recall His Past Lives renders fluid the distinction between human and animal, most explicitly in the inferred past lives of Uncle Boonmee, which return to haunt the dying man at the point of his impending passing. More generally, animals and other non-human forms are always present, invested with a cosmic significance that suggests their broad equivalence to human life, not least in terms of their potential embodiment of past and future incarnations.

As the principal site of existential transformation, the animal presence and animist possibility that inhabit the jungle setting of *Uncle Boonmee Who Can Recall His Past Lives* is significant. On the soundtrack, the ambient sounds of the jungle are given an unusually prominent position and can be heard throughout much of the film. It is part of what Philippa Lovatt describes as Apichatpong's systematic approach to haptic soundscapes and embodied aurality, whereby '"natural" ambient or environmental sounds are amplified to the extent that they become almost *denaturalized*, thus heightening their affective power' (Lovatt 2013: 62). Here, sound functions as a reminder of the other lives in the universe, and of Uncle Boonmee's path to alternative incarnation.

In this setting, animal and other non-human forms are intercut into the story of Uncle Boonmee as we encounter what we infer to be his past lives. In the pre-credit sequence, for example, establishing a life cycle that includes interspecies transmigration or reincarnation, we encounter a water buffalo that breaks free from its tether to roam through the jungle.

Later, in an instance of anthropomorphic animism, we encounter nothing less than a copulating catfish, in an interspecies aquatic-erotic liaison between a talking fish and a Thai princess – one of whom we assume to be Uncle Boonmee in a prior life.

Elsewhere, in a further interspecies encounter, an example of what James Naremore describes as 'the intercourse between spirits, animals, and humans'

Figure 4.1 A water buffalo in *Uncle Boonmee Who Can Recall His Past Lives*

Figure 4.2 A catfish in *Uncle Boonmee Who Can Recall His Past Lives*

(Naremore 2011: 35), we see Boonsong, son of Uncle Boonmee, who exists as an ape-like spirit or monkey ghost, having mated with a jungle-dwelling spirit and been transformed in the process. This entity combines the human (the capacity for speech), animal (the bodily form of a primate) and supernatural (red eyes that glow in the dark), and represents a transmogrification of sorts – both interspecies and across the threshold of natural and supernatural – resulting from a process of rebirth that is not contingent on death. In other words, Boonsong has been existentially transformed but has not died in the process.

Figure 4.3 A monkey ghost in *Uncle Boonmee Who Can Recall His Past Lives*

In this animist universe, we encounter countless animal and other non-human forms, among them bees that provide Uncle Boonmee succour; dogs that wander his farm; insects that are swatted as they fly towards the light; and bugs that are crushed underfoot, accidentally or otherwise. 'I've killed a lot of bugs on my farm', remarks Uncle Boonmee, shortly after suggesting that his kidney failure is the karmic result of having killed communists in a past conflict. In this way, a complex dynamic is established between human and animal lives, no matter how seemingly inconsequential the latter.

As insects fly around Uncle Boonmee's al fresco dining table and are occasionally illuminated by light, the crack of the zap of an electric bug trap is a recurring element of the soundtrack. Indeed, Apichatpong has recalled (in a futuristic dispatch dated 'November 6, 2552') the uncanny omnipresence of insects during the filming of this scene, or one that bears a remarkable similarity to it:

> Everything was dark. Once the lights popped up, the camera started rolling. Before the insects soared to devour the lights, we shot as much as we could. [. . .]
>
> A bug fell into a dish of fried glass noodles. His colleague followed, dropping in front of Boonmee. We halted the shooting. The men stormed the dining table with battery-operated, racquet-shaped swatters. They swiped them in the air, electrocuting, sizzling the insects. [. . .] We saw the sparks of light as the insects crackled on the electro-meshes. The light flickered. (Apichatpong 2011: unpaginated)

Consistent across all of these animal and other non-human encounters is the implied representation of Uncle Boonmee's prior lives and alternative incarnations. Anticipating the end of one materiality, past and present lives coexist in the midst of prospective existential transformation.

In each of these instances, *Uncle Boonmee Who Can Recall His Past Lives* foregrounds what Stephen Teo describes as '[t]he theme of the sociality of spirits, or the pervasiveness of spirits in nature and animals – rooted in the Buddhist belief of reincarnation' (Teo 2013: 109). The experience, he continues, 'is not of grotesque horror but of a ghostly, spiritual essence that is infusive and all around us' (Teo 2013: 109). In this schema of spiritual essence and ghostly animism, death is represented not in terms of finitude or finality, but in terms of a recurring cycle of transformation and transmigration, rebirth and reincarnation.

In looking at the ways in which *Uncle Boonmee Who Can Recall His Past Lives* explores themes of animism (see Ingawanij 2013), or at the director's recurring concern with reincarnation (see Rithdee 2009), the aim here is not to explore these ideas per se, but to suggest their metaphorical resonances with regard to the existential historiography of cinema itself and the broader notion of cinema as a form defined by its own life cycle (or cycles, plural). The intention is to map a thematic and metaphorical context for how the film's existential transformations and recollections of past lives, its emphasis on embodiment and corporeality in the context of ghostliness and spirituality, and its alternatives to a life cycle of birth and death, might be used to understand cinema with regard to its own past, present and future lives, precisely as its materially embodied – that is, filmic – incarnation meets its own moment of finitude.

Photochemical Phantasms

Cinema, too, has the ability to materially preserve past lives. It returns these photochemical phantasms to the present as mnemonic traces with ghostly resonance. If *Uncle Boonmee Who Can Recall His Past Lives* is a transmigratory portrait of the past lives and bodies of Uncle Boonmee, it is also an invocation of the past lives and bodies of cinema, as manifest in the archival corpus of filmic representations and the materiality of the medium of physical film. It is a corporeal embodiment of the soul of cinema and its indexical (that is, photochemical) relationship with the past. Allied with its existential framework of transmigration and reincarnation, the ostensibly supernatural themes of *Uncle Boonmee Who Can Recall His Past Lives* and its series of ghostly entities and hauntings offer a thematic context for, and corollary of, our understanding of cinema, its apparatus and the phantasmatic qualities of cinematic representation.

On the level of narrative, we inhabit a world in which the dead coexist with the living. As well as the return of Uncle Boonmee's past lives and the supernatural visitation of his long-lost son (now a monkey ghost) Boonsong, we also encounter Uncle Boonmee's long-dead wife, Huay, who returns as a ghost to

Figure 4.4 The ghostly visitation of Boonmee's wife in *Uncle Boonmee Who Can Recall His Past Lives*

take care of her dying husband, and who likewise hovers on the edge of existential and corporeal states.

When these spectral pasts return, in a story about death as well as commemoration and memory, they also suggest the phantasm of cinematic representation itself. In this respect, the film calls to mind what J. Hoberman has described more generally as 'a particular cinematic uncanny, in which historically self-conscious ghost movies are set in places haunted by movies' (Hoberman 2012: 20). It is a Freudian uncanny that runs counter to the treatment of ghosts in *Uncle Boonmee Who Can Recall His Past Lives* and serves as an alternative cultural conception of the ghostly that is less rooted in the *unheimlich*. Revealingly, Hoberman's exemplar is the Hollywood film noir *Sunset Boulevard* (Billy Wilder, 1950), which was 'made in the late afternoon – the magic hour – of the studio system' (Hoberman 2012: 20), paralleling the recent magic hour of a mode of cinema rooted in photochemical film. If *Uncle Boonmee Who Can Recall His Past Lives* does not represent a place haunted by movies as explicitly as *Sunset Boulevard*, it is nevertheless haunted by movies that emerge in countless referential allusions and other reflexive devices.

These hauntings, and a specific concern with ontological uncanniness, reside in the realm that Jacques Derrida has termed 'hauntology' (Derrida 1994 [1993]), which when applied to cinema locates the spectral as a cultural response to technological change, among other factors. This change is a recurring presence in *Uncle Boonmee Who Can Recall His Past Lives*, ultimately suggesting an acceptance of the spirits that represent an ontological uncertainty, as opposed to the end-of-history gloom that more typically marks the hauntological. Mark Fisher refers to a central feature of Derrida's conception of hauntology with respect to memory and time, pointing out that '[o]ne of the repeated phrases in [Derrida's] *Specters of Marx* is from *Hamlet*, "the time is out of joint"' (Fisher 2012: 18). This notion identifies, as one possibility of the hauntological, an out-of-joint return of the past into the present and a related ontological misalignment, by which the materiality of the present (ontology) is replaced by the spectral return (hauntology) of a phantasmatic trace of the past.

With regard to a historically recontextualised, reconfigured and demateri-alised cinematic apparatus, the meanings associated with photochemical film, in particular, have necessarily assumed altered historicity. In the context of increasing obsolescence, the medium of film, especially 16mm formats, carries altered signification. Film has taken on new meaning precisely in the context of its implied extinction or disappearance.

As the likes of José van Dijck remind us, media and materials necessar-ily influence both the content of films and our understanding of cinematic and other institutions of memory whereby the presence of photochemical film in an otherwise largely digital landscape complicates our understanding of cultural memory and film history. For van Dijck, such mediation can be thought of in terms of 'mediated memories' (van Dijck 2007) – memories, in the instance of *Uncle Boonmee Who Can Recall His Past Lives*, that are medi-ated via photochemical film.

Domietta Torlasco argues that the cinematic past in whatever form has con-tinued resonance, and that '[t]he rebirth of cinema, assuming that cinema has died and that it has done so only once, would lie in the discovery (never to become exhaustive) of its multiple, conflicting, hardly lived pasts' (Torlasco 2013: i). If Torlasco's principal concern is with how digital media might rework the cinematic (and largely filmic) archive, a media archaeological understand-ing of these lived pasts might also be enacted through a reflexive, comparative discovery of film formats and histories.

In *Uncle Boonmee Who Can Recall His Past Lives*, conjuring the lived pasts of cinema and equating film and reincarnation on the level of materiality, there is a broader sense of the returning memory of prior cinematic forms, Thai or otherwise, but always specific to 16mm film, which is referenced through a series of stylistic and other allusions. Awareness of the cinematic archive emerges in *Uncle Boonmee Who Can Recall His Past Lives*, as it materially engages – or mediates, in van Dijck's terms – returning incarnations of his-torical cinematic forms via the persistence of cultural memory rooted in the historical materiality of 16mm film formats.

Thai cinema, in particular, is referenced in a number of ways, excavating the past lives of historical cinematic forms as sites of personal and collec-tive cultural memory, enabling a form of reincarnation or reanimation of the cinematic corpus. Though it is not always easy to discern the discrete forms of these past lives, Apichatpong has described how each of the six reels of *Uncle Boonmee Who Can Recall His Past Lives* is shot in the distinct style of a different genre in the history of Thai cinema. 'If you care to look', he explains, 'each reel of the film has a different style – acting style, lighting style, or cinematic references' (Peranson and Rithdee 2010: 44). Linking form and content, there is a slippage between past lives – diegetic and non-diegetic, fictional and historical – wherein what is recalled are the past lives of cinema as much as those of Uncle Boonmee.

In terms of form, marking the materiality of medium as well as style, these collective cinematic references also mark a reflexive media archaeology rooted in the realm of cultural memory associated with 16mm film. As Angela O'Hara has noted, this is one of a number of Apichatpong films that engage a materially borne cultural mnemonics, exhuming a so-called golden age of Thai cinema rooted in the particularities of 16mm film:

> In the 1960s, the Thai government levied a tax on Hollywood film imports. The result was an explosion of Thai films in the 1960s and 1970s, mostly cheap action films critically referred to as *nam nouw* (stinking water); their fantastical and even nonsensical plotlines are rich terrain to many contemporary Thai filmmakers. (O'Hara 2012: 181)

Apichatpong is one of these contemporary Thai filmmakers,[4] and his decision to shoot *Uncle Boonmee Who Can Recall His Past Lives* on Super 16mm film can be seen as a deliberate effort to recall this historical era of 16mm films and its cultural memory and associated material aesthetics, now obsolete.

Notably, the allusions in *Uncle Boonmee Who Can Recall His Past Lives* are specific to 16mm film as a medium, rather than to cinema more generally, and extend to Thai television, recalling an era in which 16mm film was the principal televisual recording format in Thailand. For example, Apichatpong's supernatural monkey ghosts, with their ape-like costumes and glowing red eyes, reference historical television productions that used 16mm film. 'I was old enough to catch the television shows that used to be shot on 16mm film', he explains, routing this cinematic-televisual history through personal memories of Thai cultural history and the televisual images captured on 16mm film.

> They were done in studios with strong, and direct lighting. The lines were whispered to the actors, who mechanically repeated them. The monsters were always in the dark in order to hide the cheaply made costumes. Their eyes were red lights so that the audience could spot them. (Apichatpong 2010: unpaginated)

In this recollection of a prior era of moving images, the medium of production, 16mm film, is foregrounded.

Apichatpong's use of Super 16mm film in particular, emphasises the distinctive qualities of the medium, including the more general mnemonic properties of film (compared to digital images) rooted in a particular texture and the meanings and aesthetics associated with it. As Lucy Fife Donaldson explains, '[c]elluloid is a delicate surface that is easily marked, scratched or added to, actions which hold a range of meaning' (Fife Donaldson 2014: 34). Whereas, she continues, '[t]oo much texture is an unwanted sign of age, mishandling or lack of care, which spoils the clarity of the image' (Fife Donaldson 2014: 35), it is also the case, as with *Uncle Boonmee Who Can Recall His Past Lives*, that '[g]rain can be used expressively [. . .] which links us back to seeing the past more generally as "textured" and the passage of time enacting an erosion of the clarity of our views of it' (Fife Donaldson 2014: 36).

The materiality and physicality of film also carry unique associations with death and decay. As Stephen Barber has argued,

> film images, across filmic history, appeared complicit with their own decay and downfall, and how that content relates to conceptions of film as comprising a sensitized medium for human memory and history [. . .] The memory of film remains so embedded within the nature of memory itself that the 'lapsing', shattering or disappearance of film constitutes a significant trauma of memory, within a contemporary era that predominantly formulates visual media of oblivion. (Barber 2010: 8–9)

The texture of film, in a contemporary context, thus becomes, to return to Fisher's discussion of Derrida, a hauntological signifier – akin, for example, to the meanings associated with crackle in a sonic context, in terms of the extraneous noise associated with analogue media such as vinyl. As Fisher notes of contemporary music, the markers of a returning past are particularly evident in sounds of degradation, delay, distortion and, in 'one of sonic hauntology's signature traits, the conspicuous use of crackle, which renders time as an audible materiality' (Fisher 2012: 18). Further, he adds elsewhere, '[c]rackle makes us aware that we are listening to a time that is out of joint; it won't allow us to fall into the illusion of presence' (Fisher 2014: 21). In terms of cinema, the same can be said of the texture of film, as in the instance of *Uncle Boonmee Who Can Recall His Past Lives*. These significations are cultural rather than essential, and they hint at a particular historical claim of photochemical film with regard to its ability to record and thus preserve the past via the indexicality or ontology of the photographic and in turn cinematic image.

Cinema has a uniquely complex relationship with memory and with past lives, bound up in large part in the materiality of film and its photochemical relationship with the bodies it records and thus preserves at the point of film-ing, and which it subsequently summons as if from the dead at the point of projection. For Thomas Elsaesser, such concerns were especially marked at the turn of the twentieth century, and returned at the turn of the twenty-first, paralleling discourses of technological change, retrospectively framed in terms of moments of birth (twentieth century) and death (twenty-first century). He suggests 'thinking of cinema as the script of life in the form of *index* and *trace*, i.e., as an analog medium' (Elsaesser 2012: 590). Meanwhile, for Markos Hadjioannou, 'where film's photographic foundation encourages an existen-tial association between subject and reality through the screened image, digital depictions are graphic renditions of mathematical codes whose causal relations are more difficult to trace' (Hadjioannou 2012: ix–x).

If there is a remarkable continuity of concerns with cinema's function as index and trace, for Elsaesser, across moments of profound technological change, film as an analogue medium also now exists in the context of the prevailing digi-tal media. In its narrative of existential association between subject and reality as well as of ontology and hauntology, past lives and their ghostly return, and in its filmically mediated reflection on the relationship between embodied materiali-ties and disembodied phantasms, *Uncle Boonmee Who Can Recall His Past Lives* engages film as a medium with the ability to embalm time, preserve lives and conjure these photochemical phantasms into the present.

In certain respects, the very nature of cinema and its apparatus is ghostly. For O'Hara, Apichatpong 'is possessed by the modern melancholia that has infected the arts in this past century in the West: the haunted realm between corporeality, subjectivity, and its allegorization through the phantasm of rep-resentation' (O'Hara 2012: 180), a phantasm she further describes in terms of 'the inherently animistic characteristic of the medium of cinema as spiri-tual "medium"' (O'Hara 2012: 178). Apichatpong, for his part, articulates this haunted realm or spiritual medium thus:

> The cinema itself is like a coffin with bodies, sitting still, as if under a spell. The moving images on the screen are camera records of events that have already taken place; they are remains of the past, strung together and called a film. In this hall of darkness, ghosts are watching ghosts. (Apichatpong 2009 [2007]: 113)

With regard to the second set of ghosts, this notion suggests the memo-rial capacity that resides in photographic and cinematographic ontology. In existential terms, cinema is a realm of the eternal, those who are captured in life, preserved forevermore via photochemical film and its assumed ontology or indexicality. In the return of the past lives of Uncle Boonmee, the sugges-tion is that in the realm of cinema, too, the past persists into the present, in the form of lives that are filmed and frozen, preserved via the memorialising power of film.

It is this quality that Bazin described as 'embalming the dead' (Bazin 1960 [1945]: 4), a process of mummification that constitutes 'the preservation of life by a representation of life' (Bazin 1960 [1945]: 5). In this process, in Mary Ann Doane's terms, 'an etching or a trace' (Doane 2002: 41) of the past might also exist in the present, a preservation of past lives whose return constitutes a haunting, a combination, for Laura Mulvey, of 'the index and the uncanny' (Mulvey 2006: 54–66), which preserves 'associations with life after death' (Mulvey 2006: 54). Put another way, for Friedrich Kittler, '[o]nce memories and dreams, the dead and ghosts, become technically reproducible, readers and writers no longer need the powers of hallucination' (Kittler 1999 [1986]: 10). Considered in these terms, photochemical film, as a technically reproducible material medium, carries a trace of the past that is fundamentally phantasmatic.

Mulvey engages notions of rebirth and resurrection that are directly relevant to *Uncle Boonmee Who Can Recall His Past Lives*, arguing that

> the presence of the past in the cinema is also the presence of the body resurrected and these images can trigger, if only by association, questions that still seem imponderable: the nature of time, the fragility of human life and the boundary between life and death. (Mulvey 2006: 53)

In *Uncle Boonmee Who Can Recall His Past Lives*, memories, however ghostly, serve as a trigger for such questions including the past lives of cinema. The resonances of memory – of past lives still perceptible or tangible in the present – are also those of cinema, and of the materiality of photochemical film whose embodied memories are of cinema in general. This emphasis on materiality and embodiment reminds us that cinema also has a legacy of material embodiment – a body of sorts – that now faces a dematerialisation related to the replacement of physical film by digital formats. As cinema itself finds new incarnations, its filmic pasts return as ghosts that might coexist with the living, suggesting a continuing legacy for a materiality that is no longer material.

Transmigratory Materialities

If film can memorialise past lives, it is subject, like Uncle Boonmee, to its own potential transmigration or reincarnation, but in the face of seeming obsolescence. The concern with death and dying in *Uncle Boonmee Who Can Recall His Past Lives* applies to both Uncle Boonmee and a particular type of cinema and its medium: photochemical film in general, and 16mm film formats in particular. Apichatpong's homage to the memory and past incarnations of cinema equates the passing of Uncle Boonmee with a certain mode or

conception of cinema, and the dying human body with the corporeality of celluloid, foregrounding the moment of material-to-immaterial transition. That
is, constructing a dynamic between film and the alternative of digital, *Uncle
Boonmee Who Can Recall His Past Lives* explores the properties of film at the
specific juncture of transition between the implied physicality or materiality
of one medium and the implied non-physicality or immateriality of its digital
replacement.

Film continues to experience its own existential transformation, as it is
increasingly replaced by digital formats. Writing in 2007, D. N. Rodowick
offered 'an elegy for film' (Rodowick 2007: 90–3). Little more than a decade
later, countless critics have noted the near-universal shift to post-filmic
formats. For example, Gaudreault and Marion argue that '[t]he wane of
35mm film, long foretold but not easy to imagine, has thus now become a
cold, hard reality' (Gaudreault and Marion 2015 [2013]: 3), concluding that
'[t]he deed is done. Celluloid is dead (or almost)' (Gaudreault and Marion
2015 [2013]: 147).

Placing this shift from film to digital in existential-historiographic terms,
the imminent obsolescence of film as anything other than a specialist format
exists as a mnemonic signifier in *Uncle Boonmee Who Can Recall His Past Lives*,
linked to the themes of death and reincarnation.

As Uncle Boonmee anticipates the end of one life, leaving one bodily form
and transitioning into the next, the concern with corporeal embodiment, decay
and transmigration or reincarnation finds parallel expression in the plight of
physical film. As an inscription of the mutability of the corpus, the gradual loss
of a filmic base and the implicit degradation of cinema have become signifiers
for a broader conception of death – for example, in Susan Sontag's famous
discussion of 'the decay of cinema' (Sontag 1996), in which the metaphor of
corporeal decay offers broader existential-historiographic meaning.

For Paolo Cherchi Usai, the physical erosion of the cinematic archive that
might be thought of as a collective corpus constitutes an existential threat,
given the fragility of film and archival anxieties concerning its preservation.
In a book bluntly entitled *The Death of Cinema*, Cherchi Usai outlines his own
take on the metaphor of a natural life cycle for cinema. In his prognosis, he
describes 'the processes of decay' (Cherchi Usai 2001: 107) that mark the ageing of photochemical film and 'the indicators of the process (patina, material
and narrative gaps, colour fading, sound degradation)' (Cherchi Usai 2001:
107). Here, Usai is more precise than Sontag, suggesting a correlation between
the decay of the body and the mortality of cinema, equating the decay of film
with death itself.

Engaging such existential metaphors and historiographic discourses, *Uncle
Boonmee Who Can Recall His Past Lives* implicates film by way of a bodily
inscribed, materially mediated ontology. Allan Cameron, discussing the

relationship between filmic ontology and cinematic mediation via the representation of bodily decay in the zombie genre, suggests that '[t]he weaving
together of media and bodily metaphors' (Cameron 2012: 69) foregrounds 'the
body's ontological and phenomenological connections with media' (Cameron
2012: 67). Caetlin Benson-Allott, with reference to cinematic representations
and the ontology of celluloid, contends that films have the capacity to ask 'the
spectator to look beyond the content of the frame and contemplate the philosophical implications of an image's material relationship with its substrate'
(Benson-Allott 2013: 173). *Uncle Boonmee Who Can Recall His Past Lives*
addresses this concern in that it foregrounds the formal properties associated
with the passing of its medium. That is, in the same way that the body of
Uncle Boonmee fails, the corpus of cinema will fail, too, with the materiality of
photochemical film – and of 16mm formats in particular – a key signification
of this process.

In this allegorical narrative, the death of Uncle Boonmee is framed in
terms of the fragility and decay of the dying man's body, pending transmigration or reincarnation, and as a journey into the unknown via a symbolic,
liminal landscape in which rebirth is implied. Setting off towards his even-
tual passing, Uncle Boonmee journeys through the jungle as if on a ritual
procession. For Ingawanij, in animism, the jungle as the site where humans
metamorphose 'into animal form signifies the possibility of freedom or the
preservation of the essence of self' (Ingawanij 2013: 94). In *Uncle Boonmee
Who Can Recall His Past Lives*, if the precise form of metamorphosis has still
to be determined, the jungle will nevertheless function as the site of Uncle
Boonmee's existential transition.

The destination of Uncle Boonmee's journey is a jungle cave in which he will
end his life. In the darkness of this cave, there are few signs of life except the fish
that swim in a rock pool – thematically and visually evoking the earlier catfish.
The monkey ghosts that will soon gather at the cave's periphery are a reminder
of the film's multi-species existential ecosystem and the possibility of human–
animal transformation. Meanwhile, the prehistoric carvings on the cave's walls
serve as a pre-cinematic visual marker, a physical and symbolic inscription of the
cycle of life, cinematic and other, which predates and will postdate the present
physical incarnations of Uncle Boonmee and cinema alike.

In this resting place, Uncle Boonmee invokes a recurring cycle of life, defined
by animist possibility: 'This cave . . . It's like a womb, isn't it?' At the very point
of death, it is the womb, that site of nurtured birth, which is symbolically suggested. This cave will serve, as James Quandt notes, 'as both Boonmee's womb
and his tomb' (Quandt 2011: 60). In the cave, Uncle Boonmee reminds us that
'I was born here in a life I can't recall', suggesting both the existence of past lives
and the slippages between forms: 'I don't know if I was a human or an animal,
a woman or a man . . .'

In the larger context of cinematic representation and evolving technology, it is significant that it is a cave – suggesting Plato's allegory of the cave and the shadows cast on its walls[5] – in which Uncle Boonmee will end his life. This space of darkness illuminated by the occasional shaft of light – a projection of sorts – is not only a womb and tomb, it is also a surrogate for cinema.

Indeed, the womb has been used as a metaphor for cinema, with the cinematic apparatus itself constructed, in psychoanalytic terms, as a return to the womb, a connection suggested by Jean-Louis Baudry, who also likened cinema to the light that illuminated the wall of Plato's cave, which represents 'the whole apparatus' (Baudry 1976 [1975]: 109) of cinema, from the 'projector' (Baudry 1976 [1975]: 109) to 'the wall-screen' (Baudry 1976 [1975]: 109) and its image.

Echoing Baudry, Apichatpong has outlined his own reflexive account, providing a new context for Plato in theorising the relationship between cave, womb and cinema. 'Just as we like to look at ghosts', he suggests, 'we seem instinctively to want to enter dark halls; we are excited by the prospect of hearing stories that emanate from that light in the darkness. It is like returning to our mother's womb, fleeing there for safety' (Apichatpong 2009 [2007]: 114). The cave is framed as a site intimately associated with cinema, with a broader cycle of birth and death. Apichatpong constructs what Naremore calls a 'cinema cave [. . .] dedicated to recovering a repressed history, healing pain, and connecting our spirits with others' (Naremore 2011: 37).

In *Uncle Boonmee Who Can Recall His Past Lives*, death can be seen within a macro-historical context of a returning repressed history and its relationship with the future. While in this cave, Uncle Boonmee dreams a vision as if foreseeing a future life or travelling back in time from a future incarnation, whose memories remain. Over a succession of photographic images that reference those in Chris Marker's *The Jetty* (*La jetée*, 1962), a film that principally comprises still images and concerned with similar themes of memory and medium, Uncle Boonmee recounts his own mnemonic encounter. In this cinematic vision of the future, via the pre-cinematic form of photography, the circularity of time is formally and thematically articulated, and cinema is figured as a means of time travel, through lives and incarnations past, present and future.

Soon after this vision, Uncle Boonmee's death is inferred. We cut from the cave at night to the cave by day, via a series of shots of a junglescape that collectively elide the precise moment of Uncle Boonmee's passing, and which pave the way for his implied reincarnation into an alternative form.

In the jungle cave as a symbolic space of existential transformation, the dying body of Uncle Boonmee and the collective traces of his past lives are reminders of the materiality of the cinematic apparatus and the medium of film. The death of Uncle Boonmee is also a media-metaphorical death, in

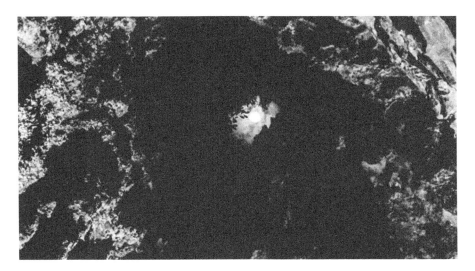

Figures 4.5–4.6 Cave by night (top) and day (bottom) in *Uncle Boonmee Who Can Recall His Past Lives*

which the corpus of Uncle Boonmee is equated with the cinematic body precisely at a moment of transition out of its present physical form with past lives recalled at the moment of existential transition. Linking memory, history and death, the materiality of film thus bridges the past and present, formally enunciating a historical moment in which the end of a certain type of cinema, and its material base, are both narrativised and visually inscribed. Connecting this narrative of death to a broader existential historiography, film is positioned as but one body for the soul or spirit of cinema, as the borders between life and death, film and digital, are invoked and crossed.

CONCLUSION

If *Uncle Boonmee Who Can Recall His Past Lives* seeks to memorialise the past – the life of Uncle Boonmee (incarnate in human form) in the fiction, and that of a particular type of cinema (incarnate in photochemical film) beyond the fiction – it is also reflexively aware of how notions of birth and death might help us conceptualise and understand the existential transformations of cinema today. Beyond the cave, beyond death, what next for Uncle Boonmee? And, with an existential-historiographic life cycle as a broader backdrop, what next for cinema?

For Apichatpong, the story of cinema need not end at the so-called death or obsolescence of photochemical film. As the multiple lives of Uncle Boonmee remind us, a narrative of death might also be one of rebirth; a story of life might also incorporate one or more afterlives. In other words, the mnemonic resonances of past embodiments suggests the possibility of future lives. Technological change does not constitute death as a singular and absolute moment of finitude, but rather a natural phase in an ongoing life cycle.

The cycle that *Uncle Boonmee Who Can Recall His Past Lives* constructs as Uncle Boonmee experiences his passing in the mnemonic midst of past lives, is also the story of film as a medium. The metaphorical body of celluloid is signified in terms of the distinctive visual texture and signifiers of Super 16mm and is one of the metaphorical incarnations – water buffalo, catfish, monkey ghost and many others – that cinema might materially inhabit in its own cycle of rebirth, reincarnation or transmigration. In this narrative, Boonmee inhabits human as well as non-human forms as part of a seemingly endless cycle of birth, death and reincarnation. Applied to cinema, as the medium of film becomes increasingly obsolete, it is a passing life that anticipates future lives with a more fluid conception of film, as an art, as the soul or spirit that transcends the corporeal form of a dying medium, in much the same way that the soul or spirit of Uncle Boonmee transitions from one life to the next, one body to the next.

Francesco Casetti argues that

> [a] self is an opening to the other. It is such an identity that in the past allowed cinema to remain itself even when it adopted new guises. It is such an identity that today allows cinema, threatened by more radical modifications, to continue on its path. (Casetti 2015: 8)

In engaging the very nature of cinema at a time of such radical modifications, or transmigrating materialities, *Uncle Boonmee Who Can Recall His Past Lives* conjures the past lives of cinema itself, while also asking us to imagine new ones – as remarkable, perhaps, as the animal and other forms of Uncle Boonmee.

3D Images at the Edge of History: *Goodbye to Language* and *The Three Disasters*

Extending an existential historiography, this chapter explores how shifts in technology – in this instance, experiments in 3D – might both engage the cinematic archive in one historical direction, while simultaneously seeking to reimagine the very nature of cinema in the other. If shifts in technology raise questions of obsolescence with regard to extant forms, they also offer new means to engage and reframe – literally and otherwise – conceptions of film history and collective cultural memory. This chapter proposes the renewal of cinema to be contingent on continued historical awareness, with a cine-literate – or even cinephilic – cognisance of film history an essential part of any contemporary – or future, for that matter – reimagining.

In terms of an evolving film history and how these moments of technological change might be theorised, it could be useful to consider the broader historical dynamics of the contemporary re-emergence of 3D and the resonance of its own past incarnations as they relate to the cinematic present. In this sense, experiments with 3D cinema, in particular, raise a series of larger questions: What, for example, might the recent return of 3D mean for the future of cinema? In terms of comparing both cinematic images and their underlying apparatuses, what might close analysis of 3D and 2D images tell us about the distinctive aesthetics and other specificities associated with these historically overlapping representational modes? And ultimately, what might the renewed interest in 3D cinema reveal about the history of cinema as a whole?

In the realm of a technologically mediated film historiography, in which mortal metaphors of departure question even the continued existence of cinema, there is arguably no better case study than veteran French filmmaker Jean-Luc Godard. Godard has long been associated with the fundamental relationships between technology, history and aesthetics, however complex or critical, from the starting point of a committed cinephilia. If, in fact, technological change holds the capacity to rupture or even destroy cinema, this same technology holds the concomitant potential to reinvent, that is, to stave off potential obsolescence through regenerative transformation. Accordingly, for Godard, a still resonant film history is explored via the technologies and representational modes of the present as a means to reflect on the broader status of cinema and its cumulative history precisely within and through the contemporary historical moment.

Godard's recent 3D films ask the viewer to attend to this changing technology and its consequences for cinema, with the aim of redefining the medium and our understanding of its history. Put simply: technologies uniquely enable us to see the world anew, including the existing corpus of the cinematic archive, and in the hands of Godard, 3D exemplifies this capability. As this chapter will analyse in detail, such reflexive engagement with technological change – framed in terms of a dialectic of finality on the one hand, and renewal on the other – has been a decades-long concern of the director, which finds new form as articulated via 3D cinema.

GOODBYE TO LANGUAGE AND THE THREE DISASTERS: FILM HISTORY IN THE X-, Y- AND Z- DIMENSIONS

'I am going to die. *Adieu, adieu.*'[1]
– Josette (Héloïse Godet), *Goodbye to Language*
(*Adieu au langage*, 2014)[2]

'When I say "adieu" to language, I mean "adieu" to my own way of speaking, which cinema still allows.'
– Jean-Luc Godard, *In Conversation with Jean-Luc Godard*
(Cécile Mella, 2014)

In saying *adieu* to one particular cinematic way of speaking through a reflexive historiography of 3D images that exist at the very edge of film history, Godard's debut 3D feature film, *Goodbye to Language*,[3] and its closely related 3D short, *The Three Disasters* (*Les trois désastres*, 2013), collectively engage the possibilities of 3D cinema to address their consequences for cinema in general. Specifically, in linking notions of death and departure, in narrative as well as linguistic, formal and historiographic concerns, the very language of cinema – the *langage* of *Goodbye to Language* – is reimagined precisely at the moment of its perceived farewell – its *adieu*.

In adopting and adapting a 3D apparatus, and in Godard's creative uses of this technology,[4] *Goodbye to Language* and *The Three Disasters* extend a career-long approach to technological change, in terms of a broader concern with film history. At a moment of actual or potential transition,[5] technology is utilised to communicate a self-inscribed history or historiography of cinema. Foregrounding the apparatus and aesthetics of 3D filmmaking,[6] Godard explores perspectival imaging and spatialised perception in films that interrogate the technological possibilities and linguistic conventions of 3D cinema, all the while in a complex dynamic of exchange with the largely (if not exclusively) 2D cinematic past. The result is twinned films that use the technologies of the present to navigate the history of cinema, as well as vice versa.

In representing this history, a dialectical approach to technology mirrors, maps and mediates Godard's reflection on the continued vitality (or otherwise) of cinema and the potential for technological, aesthetic and artistic renewal. Reworking the director's continuing concern with the limits of cinema and the conditions of its re-articulation, this end-of-history or end-of-cinema *adieu* negotiates a broader context of finitude and obsolescence. Consistent with long-standing proclamations of nothing less than the death (or deaths, plural) of cinema, *Goodbye to Language* and *The Three Disasters* delineate a spatialised historiography that addresses the present plight of this medium. Cinema is positioned, in this formulation, simultaneously at the point of existential demise and its potential concomitant rebirth or reinvention, with the technologies and aesthetics of 3D imaging positioned as one means of reframing cinema, both literally and metaphorically.

Cinema's Long Adieu

In adopting 3D in the specific context of an articulated *adieu*, *Goodbye to Language* and *The Three Disasters* represent the latest iteration of Godard's uniquely technological-eschatological approach to technological change, by which the director has historically embraced precisely those technologies that might bring about the death of cinema, at least in its existing form. Technology and eschatology are inextricably linked in this most recent *adieu*, with discourses of death – arguably, the ultimate *adieu* – a recurring element of his understanding of cinema and its potential reinvention. According to this dialectic – or 'paradox', as Serge Daney has termed Godard's quest to 'come to terms with both the "death" of cinema and its future metamorphoses' (Daney 2007 [1986]: 70) – far from simply resisting the contemporary re-emergence of 3D cinema, *Goodbye to Language* and *The Three Disasters* adopt and reorient those technologies under scrutiny, breathing new life into cinema even while pronouncing a passing or announcing an *adieu*.

Indeed, at first glance, 3D would seem to be a curious choice for Godard, filmmaking pioneer of the French *nouvelle vague* (new wave) of the 1960s. After all, if there is a long cinematic history of experimentation with 3D (for a useful overview, see Balsom 2015), this technology or mode of representation has hitherto been used principally for novelty and spectacle – in the B-movies of the 1950s, for example, and, in a latter-day renaissance, the blockbusters of recent years. Traditionally, 3D cinema has existed within an industrial framework of special effects and spectacular entertainment, described by James Quandt, in the contemporary realm, as a 'mania for the gimmick' (Quandt 2014: 127). For Ariel Rogers, likewise, the appeal of contemporary digital 3D cinema, as a variation on the emergence of 3D and its marketing in the 1950s, is rooted in 'the spectacular attraction of new technologies' (Rogers 2013: 180), or, linking past and present, what André Gaudreault and Philippe Marion describe as cinema's contemporary 'return to the days of the "big spectacle" (which is precisely what it is in the process of doing with the powerful return of 3D and the proliferation of extravaganzas)' (Gaudreault and Marion 2015 [2013]: 14).

By contrast, Godard's 3D cinema offers no such spectacle. If David Bordwell reminds us that the more typical role of 3D is 'to awe us with special effects' (Bordwell 2014), critic A. O. Scott notes of *Goodbye to Language* that

> [t]here are none of the usual special effects to be seen here: Mr. Godard has no interest in capturing the magic of flight or making monsters seem real. Instead, the everyday world is made vivid and strange, rendered in a series of sketches and compositions by an artist with an eccentric and unerring eye. (Scott 2014: 5)

For fellow critic Amy Taubin, too, there is '[n]o surprise, Godard isn't interested in making us think we can touch the fingers that seem to reach out from the surface of the screen' (Taubin 2014: 49). Rather, Godard reorients the apparatus and language of a 3D filmmaking tradition that has favoured realism as opposed to abstraction.

Yet as Daney reminds us, Godard also has a decades-long history of consciously engaging new technology in order to interrogate its fundamental characteristics, with 3D the most recent iteration of this reflexive approach to technological change. Drawing attention to the apparatus, Godard sets the stage, in part, for the comparative analysis of 3D and 2D images, technologies and modes of representation. This is, after all, the perennial search for the discovery of a new type of cinema, and a new apparatus, that will also sustain or revivify the old.

For Daney, framing this paradox in expressly cinephilic terms, a dynamic exists between an attachment to the preservation and memorialisation of cinema on the one hand, and the desire to discover and embrace its future forms on the other, even if this means producing what Taubin has described, with regard to *Goodbye to Language*, as 'a film attuned to a future that likely will not come to pass' (Taubin 2014: 49). This distinctive approach to cinema is characterised by a quest for renewal so vigorous that it risks in its very expressions of love the fundamental transformation, and thus the potential destruction, of its love-object. As Daney describes this obsessive cinephilia,

[a] love of the cinema desires only cinema, whereas passion is excessive: it wants cinema but it also wants cinema to become something else, it even longs for the horizon where cinema risks being absorbed by dint of metamorphosis, it opens up its focus onto the unknown. (Daney 2007 [1986]: 68)

In the contemporary realm of 3D cinema, in seeking out one such unknown almost three decades after Daney's initial articulation of this quest, Godard is once again, in Daney's terms, 'caught between a recent past and a near future' (Daney 2007 [1986]: 71) in his engagement with 3D as a potential means to revivify cinema, even to the point of much cherished existing modes 'being absorbed by dint of metamorphosis' in this process.

Framed in the specific context of the discourses of death that Daney also raises, *Goodbye to Language* and *The Three Disasters* invoke an existential farewell (that is, the departure of 2D cinema) precisely via the cause of that demise (that is, the arrival or return of 3D cinema), interrogating in the process the very notion of finality at the heart of Godard's act of simultaneous cinematic mourning and resurrection.

As one example, connecting the contemporary cine-historical moment on the one hand, and the collective history of cinema and its cumulative archive of sounds and images on the other, *Goodbye to Language* at times combines a dizzyingly dense collage comprising archival footage of various kinds – from feature films to newsreels – alongside a stream of aphoristic and often gnomic philosophical and other textual quotations, presented in the form of intertitle-style graphics, alongside newly shot 3D footage. In this assemblage of episodic fragments and sensorial shards, Godard portrays a doubling narrative of theme and variation, framed around the amorous affairs of parallel couples, whose doubling neatly functions as a formal corollary of the doubling of the image – the left eye and right eye – of stereoscopy (see Thompson and Bordwell 2014).

If *Goodbye to Language* is the director's first feature-length foray into 3D filmmaking, it follows *The Three Disasters*, his contribution to the 2013 anthology film *3X3D* (comprising separate 3D shorts by Godard, Peter Greenaway and Edgar Pêra). At approximately seventeen minutes in duration, and with a Cannes premiere almost a full year prior to that of *Goodbye to Language*, *The Three Disasters* can in many respects be thought of as a standalone work. At the same time, it might productively be considered in close dialogue with *Goodbye to Language*, as a complementary or twinned work or even as a preparatory study for the later, feature-length film. Both films, for example, share an apparatus and a broad aesthetic, and much of the footage appears across both films. While noting significant variations where they exist, this chapter generally considers *Goodbye to Language* and *The Three Disasters* as constituting a collective approach to 3D cinema as well as having a shared engagement with film history more generally.

Both films, for example, extend the director's long history of bidding *adieu* to cinema in one form or another, as an integral element of the perpetual quest to sustain the medium through its technological and aesthetic transformations, even to the point of repeated proclamations of the death of cinema as a central imperative for this process (see Morgan 2012: 203–6; Witt 1999; Witt 2013: 112–34). In short, Godard is no stranger to the idea that cinema is precariously poised and subject to one or more potential deaths, a notion that recurs throughout his filmmaking career of more than half a century.

With regard to the contemporary significance of 3D in particular, it is notable that Godard's conception of death is one that is multiple rather than singular, encompassing a series of transformations – metamorphoses, in Daney's terms – as opposed to a monolithic and thus totalising conception of filmic finitude. As Michael Witt writes, 'when Godard talks of the "death" of cinema he is in fact invoking a series of quite distinct "deaths"' (Witt 1999: 331), adding that within this historiographic schema or cycle, 'the very notion of "cinema" undergoes a series of mutations' (Witt 1999: 333), with the emphasis on the plural.

Because of this plurality, Godard's proclamations of death, and now *adieu*, are not claims of absolute demise for the medium as a whole. Rather, they function as symbolic markers of the type of shift or rupture that Gaudreault and Marion describe as existential 'crises' (Gaudreault and Marion 2015 [2013]), noting how 'cinema's entire history has been punctuated by moments when its media identity has been radically called into question' (Gaudreault and Marion 2015 [2013]: 2–3). To the fore of such moments – of which the recent renaissance of 3D might be considered one, at least in combination with other factors – Godard has often identified the technological and other conditions by which the identity of cinema is questioned.

Yet, if Godard has consistently engaged such crises, he has done so not as a reactionary gesture, nor as an act of simple nostalgia, but with a view to the radical reinvention of the medium in question. For Daniel Morgan, '[e]ach time Godard announces the death of the cinema, it is with the intent of showing that a particular way of making films has ended, is no longer viable, and therefore that something new is required' (Morgan 2012: 204). Time and again, there is an emphasis on what has ended in order to establish a succession of beginnings. As Morgan continues, 'Godard arrives at an end but is able to imagine it as containing cleared ground – perhaps a new "return to zero" – on which cinema can be reestablished' (Morgan 2012: 204).

Such a dialectic – or return to zero – might account for the seeming contradiction of a film, *Goodbye to Language*, that arrives by announcing its own *adieu*, including in its very title. With regard to this implied farewell, the emphasis on the word – *adieu* – points to an impending or perhaps past departure, perhaps even that of cinema itself, including the possibility of the long *adieu* of death. In addition to the presence of the word *adieu* in the film's title and several references to death in its narrative (for example, in the implied deaths of the film's parallel male protagonists), *adieu* – as a word, idea and gesture – is also linguistically and visually foregrounded in a number of ways.

In the opening thirty seconds alone of *Goodbye to Language*, the word adieu appears no fewer than four times in the form of a repeated intertitle. In this textual opening, there is a remarkable continuity with the textual ending of Godard's *Weekend* (*Week-end*, 1967) and its closing title '*fin de cinéma*' (end of cinema), a playfully provocative but also prescient pun on the more typical '*fin*' (end) that closes many French-language films. Now, approximately fifty years later, *Goodbye to Language* begins by bidding *adieu*, a salutation or benediction most typical of departure.

Evidencing Daney's paradox, this *adieu* is communicated via the contemporary apparatus and aesthetics of 3D cinema, a largely historical mode that has nevertheless found renewed popularity in recent years in reconfigured form, now further reconfigured by Godard. In these instances, the recurring visualisation of the word *adieu* exemplifies the consistent use of 3D imaging to reframe cinema history, including the evolving history of 3D cinema itself. Establishing a formal but also historiographic dynamic, the word *adieu* is at times represented flat as if the word itself were in 2D, while at other times it is shown in 3D variations. In the latter, text is layered over text, creating a sense of depth, as if these words were floating in space on different planes. In one such instance, the word *adieu* is positioned in the foreground, overlaying a second layer of text – '*tous ceux qui manquent d'imagination se réfugient dans la réalité*' (all those who lack imagination take refuge in reality) – that becomes the background, a perspectival delineation emphasised when rendered in 3D.

There are numerous notable linguistic nuances and subtleties in the word *adieu*, which Godard also foregrounds, including in its associations with death. Following the linguistic cue of a repeated intertitle of the word *langage*, which is also contained in the film's title, we might note the particular meanings of *adieu* – as opposed, for example, to goodbye or farewell in common English translation. Moreover, *adieu* is very different from *au revoir*, in the same way that goodbye and farewell – only loose equivalents to either *adieu* or *au revoir* – have their own specific meanings. Put another way, *adieu* carries the polysemic or linguistic complexity that Godard appears to lament in his titular evocation of *langage* as articulated in the context of an *adieu*.

This linguistic complexity is reminiscent of Emmanuel Levinas (see, for example, Levinas 1986 [1982]) – and of Jacques Derrida's reading of Levinas (see, for example, Derrida 1995 [1992], 1999 [1997]) – as well as the more general polysemy of the word *adieu* and its etymological rooting. For Quandt:

> When Godard reconfigures *adieu* as AH DIEU in an intertitle, he is aware not only that *dieu* in English is contained within his own name but also that his hero Levinas considered *adieu* a crucial expression, as greeting, benediction, and farewell, the last sense culminating in death, as Derrida suggested in his Levinas eulogy, the word ultimately transforming into a last address to God (*à Dieu*). (Quandt 2014: 128)

In this context, we might ask, is Godard's the type of *adieu* that Derrida describes in *The Gift of Death* as '[t]he salutation or benediction given at the moment of separation, of departure, sometimes forever (this can never in fact be excluded), without any return on this earth, at the moment of death' (Derrida 1995 [1992]: 47)?

In reflecting on the word *adieu*, Derrida draws on the work of Levinas, a figure implicitly referenced in *Goodbye to Language* in a shot in which a character picks up one of his authored books. The word *adieu* has special significance for Levinas, for whom, as Derrida reminds us in his own *Adieu to Emmanuel Levinas* (Derrida 1999 [1997]),[7] to say *adieu*, derived from the word *dieu* (god), is to suggest an existence or presence of sorts in death, but also beyond death. As Derrida puts it, '[t]he greeting of the *à-Dieu* does not signal the end' (Derrida 1999 [1997]: 13).

In *Goodbye to Language*, Godard articulates his own *adieu* via the cine-linguistic vocabulary of 3D imaging. On several occasions, the word *adieu* is rephrased as *ah dieux* (ah gods) in a linguistic but also visual pun, with the *ah* and the *dieux* seemingly separated in space, text afore text, when rendered in 3D. That the composite syllables – *ah* and *dieux* – are represented on different planes, foregrounding the process of 3D imaging, constitutes a playful pun of course, but is also a reminder of Godard's etymological-existential (or metaphorical-metaphysical) framing of the word *adieu* as the root source of this pun. Indeed, this playful visualisation of the word god, or gods, is a pun that raises the existential ante or philosophical stakes of Godard's *adieu*. Once again, the director links the technological – in this instance, the realm of 3D imaging – with the eschatological – the question of the finality of death – in the broader context of a recurring concern with the death (and, by extension, potential resurrection) of cinema.

With regard to *adieu* as a potential synonym for death, and offering a tantalising possibility of an existential linguistics that sees death and birth residing in the exact same utterance, it is significant that *adieu* is in some respects a goodbye that is also a hello – and, by extension, a departure that is also an arrival. As Derrida has written, the word *adieu* can also be used as a greeting,

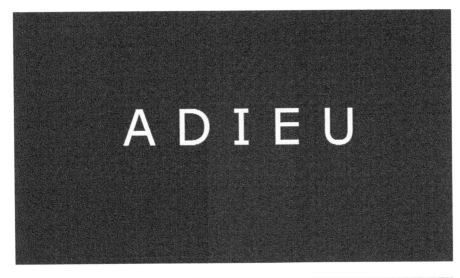

Figures 5.1–5.2 The word *adieu* (top) in a graphic that appears on several occasions in *Goodbye to Language* and as transformed into *ah dieux* (bottom)

something akin to hello. After all, as he writes in *The Gift of Death*, the multiple meanings of the word *adieu* also include:

> The salutation or benediction given (before all constative language 'adieu' can just as well signify 'hello', 'I can see you', 'I see that you are there', I speak to you before telling you anything else – and in certain circumstances in French it happens that one says *adieu* at the moment of meeting rather than separation). (Derrida 1995 [1992]: 47)

For his part, Godard likewise explains that *adieu* may mean either goodbye or hello, depending on context – such as time of day, tone of voice and French-speaking region (including Vaud, the French-speaking part of Switzerland where Godard lives and where much of *Goodbye to Language* and *The Three Disasters* were filmed). Indeed, when asked whether *adieu* is also a way of saying hello in Switzerland, Godard responded thus: 'That is in the canton of Vaud, absolutely. There are both meanings, necessarily' (Dagen and Nouchi 2014: 18; my translation).

In *Goodbye to Language* and *The Three Disasters*, implicating cinema in this linguistic meditation, we encounter the further complexity of both meanings (*les deux sens*). That is, in the context of technologies whose existence suggests the potential demise of one linguistic mode in the very utterance of another, the word *adieu* bridges the past – as a cinematic goodbye, farewell or departure – to, and via, the cinema of the present – as a cinematic greeting, welcome or arrival.

2D–3D

Beyond the multi-layered resonance of the word *adieu*, Godard positions the increasingly 3D present in dialectical exchange with a principally 2D past in his visual-linguistic concerns. In *Goodbye to Language* and *The Three Disasters*, the historical memory of cinema is invoked in a number of ways, with the distinctive properties of space, depth and dimensionality of the 3D image used to chart cine-historical relations. Here, the emphasis is on the use of contemporary technologies of representation to interrogate the broader history of cinema, including its corpus of extant sounds and images, modes of expression and semantic structures.

As Erika Balsom reminds us, 3D cinema itself – beyond any technological or technical distinction of digital or otherwise – has a long cinematic history, noting particular continuities and parallels with the 3D cinema of the early to mid-1950s, which she terms 'the so-called golden age of stereoscopic cinema' (Balsom 2015: 355). Balsom makes the case that a historical approach to 3D cinema

> opens the possibility of finding a history more continuous and complex than is often acknowledged, in which the possibilities of stereoscopy have been called on for myriad uses, many of which lie far from storytelling, beyond the regime of commodified innovation that governs Hollywood, and are, at times, even positioned against it. (Balsom 2015: 361)

Moving towards the historiographic imperative of an expanded historical frame, with regard to 3D, she suggests, 'it may be time to start thinking historically about what has come and gone' (Balsom 2015: 355), an endeavour to which Godard, on the evidence of his 3D films, seemingly subscribes.

Regardless, Godard's is not a straightforward history of the 3D image; rather, it is one that considers and complicates our understanding of 3D and 2D images alike, via his comparative analysis of the relationships between cinematic modes and dimensional perspectives. In both *Goodbye to Language* and *The Three Disasters*, the 2D image is thus explicitly situated within a 3D context, and vice versa.

As one example of a comparative approach, we can return to the use of intertitles. In several instances of layered text, perspectivally mapped between foreground and background, the 3D image is positioned in direct relation to the 2D image to which it is being compared. In *Goodbye to Language*, one especially revealing example shows the word 3D positioned directly in front of the word 2D, partly obscuring it, spatially separated by the amplified depth or parallax of the 3D image. As the word 3D – itself rendered in 3D – reminds us, to bid *adieu* to cinema is also to raise the possibility of a reframing of its history.

Also in *Goodbye to Language*, as a variation on this historiographic visualisation, the words *mémoire historique* (historical memory) are illustrated in one intertitle as if in 2D, immediately followed by an intertitle in which the word 3D is overlaid, as positioned in the foreground of the 3D image, and thus in front of and partly obscuring the original phrase, which now assumes the background. This second configuration also appears in *The Three Disasters*, though in different sequence to the preceding *mémoire historique* intertitle in *Goodbye to Language*. In the realm of cinema, these compositions suggest, to say *adieu* is to conjure the historical memory of the medium, as its history now exists vis-à-vis the contemporary re-emergence of 3D cinema.

Yet, in both films, as if to complicate a straightforward historical reading, the phrase *mémoire historique* – with the word 3D overlaid – is immediately followed by an intertitle in which the phrase is replaced by the linguistic pun *malheur historique* (historical misfortune), again partly obscured by the word 3D, in the instance of *Goodbye to Language*, positioned in dimensional relief when rendered in 3D. Linguistic associations situate Godard's concern with film history and its continuities and discontinuities, within a wider web of referential relations, philosophical allusions and entangled historicity.

Such perspectival play is part of a broader system in which past and present (or present and past) are interconnected – at times explicitly, at other times implicitly – by myriad verbal and visual citations, typically unattributed. Sources are mediated (or *re*mediated) via the 3D image, including representations of other media technologies, such as several shots depicting smartphones. An image in *Goodbye to Language* shows a man holding an iPhone, the screen of which is directed towards the camera – a frame within the frame – and thus towards the wider framing of the cinema frame or screen from which the iPhone appears to extend by way of the emergent properties of the 3D image. The iPhone's own screen-based interface (displaying a web source on philosopher Jacques Ellul, notable in part for his own questioning of the role of technology and its impact on humanity) constitutes a double mediation. The iPhone as book is the first mediation, with the second being the iPhone screen as mediated by the film frame and its 3D perspectival processing, including of the countless literary and philosophical sources quoted and alluded to elsewhere in the film.

Charting alternative 3D–2D (or 2D–3D) relations, a number of archival moving images – almost exclusively from 2D sources – are intercut with the films' newly shot 3D footage, further complicating these already densely layered collages of media forms. Numerous feature films are excerpted, including Jean-Pierre Melville's *The Strange Ones* (*Les Enfants terribles*, 1950) and Howard Hawks's *Only Angels Have Wings* (1939) among others, as are archival newsreels and contemporary television footage. The result is a comparative mapping of moving images that span decades and dimensions alike.

Such references, considered as cinematic homages or acts of memorialisation, have become a signature of the so-called late-Godard period of the director's work (see, for example, Fox 2018; Morgan 2012; Witt 2013), perhaps most explicitly in *(Hi)story(ies) of Cinema* (*Histoire(s) du cinéma*, 1988–1998), a film that is itself briefly excerpted in *Goodbye to Language* and *The Three Disasters* on several occasions, encouraging such connections. As Witt argues of the late-Godard enshrining of film history, '[i]f the cinema is dead, Godard's late work is a graveyard, peppered with image-tombstones of those who have "died in action"' (Witt 1999: 334). If *Goodbye to Language* and *The Three*

Figure 5.3 *Only Angels Have Wings* as excerpted in *Goodbye to Language*

Disasters might each be thought of as an image-tombstone of sorts, they more literally memorialise those who have died in action, in Witt's terms, in the form of their archival historical footage and excerpted film clips, which are intercut with newly shot material.

For Florence Jacobowitz and Richard Lippe, this referencing of film history 'suggests that Godard is acknowledging his long term commitment to these filmmakers who use narrative cinema to comment on the personal and social world' (Jacobowitz and Lippe 2015: 24). While such acknowledgement is certainly in line with Godard's long-avowed cinephilia, these cinematic references also function in more complex ways.

In terms of reflexive historiography, for example, in *The Three Disasters*, as one playfully self-aware homage, filmmakers Nicholas Ray and John Ford are referenced in the form of photographic portraits, a gesture that goes well beyond simple allusion. Photographic images of the directors (Ray at the fore, Ford at the rear) bookend an extended shot of the custom-rigged twin-camera 3D set-up that Godard used in the production of this film – including this very shot – as well as in *Goodbye to Language* (see Corfield 2014). These twinned left-eye and right-eye cameras record the composite left-eye and right-eye images that together constitute the stereoscopically processed 3D image.

The images of Ray and Ford, beyond their cine-historical significance as iconic auteurs – championed, for example, by the *Cahiers du cinéma* cohort of which Godard was a part – are notable because each of these figures, both in real life and as portrayed in these portraits, suffered visual impairment and wore an

Figure 5.4 Mirrored and reflected 3D cameras in *The Three Disasters*

eye patch as a result: right eye, in the instance of Ray; left eye, in the instance of Ford. Adding to the extent to which the stereoscopy of the 3D apparatus is already at the fore, this visual pun, concerning ocular perception and the historicity of cinematic visuality, reminds us of the pairing of eyes – left eye and right eye – that constitutes the visual apparatus of the stereoscopic image that has just been represented. In this combination of shots, Godard implicitly challenges the representational convention of perspectival unity by drawing attention to the otherwise invisible construction of separate left-eye and right-eye images. He evokes a direct comparison to filmmakers for whom one eye proved more than sufficient. These filmmakers' collective stereoscopy or perspectival unity is achieved only within Godard's visual pun of the combination of composite lenses, one eye apiece, paired virtually and visually across cinematic moments and modes. Each still image of Ray and Ford is also reframed mid-shot, altering the framing in the first instance and the aspect ratio in the second, further emphasising the reflexive focus on ocular perception and visual representation.

Figures 5.5–5.6 Composite stereoscopy by way of Nicholas Ray's left eye (top) and John Ford's right eye (bottom) in *The Three Disasters*

In terms of archival moving images, meanwhile, excerpted footage is sometimes reworked (slowed down, for instance, or overlaid with sounds other than the original soundtrack of each underlying source), and in all instances recontextualised, whether formally manipulated or otherwise. At the very least, new associations are provided by the overarching framing of each 3D film and its own thematic, historiographic and other concerns. Indeed, the specific context of 3D cinema encourages the spectator to see otherwise hidden, neglected or latent aspects of depth and dimensionality in principally 2D archival sources, moving images that assume new life in a defamiliarised viewing.

In focusing on and exploring the latent depth of the otherwise flat 2D image, Godard also reminds us of the sometimes overlooked depth properties of 2D or planar cinema. If Stephen Prince, for example, situates 3D cinema within a schema of realism, which generally runs counter to Godard's anti- or counter-realist reflexive abstractions, Prince also details the depth qualities of the 2D image. As Prince explains, '[c]onventional (planar) cinema is 3D to the extent that it replicates the monocular depth cues that observers employ when viewing spatial layouts in the world at distances of six feet or more' (Prince 2012: 205), a historical property that Godard exploits on numerous occasions, by way of his 3D recontextualisations.

In one remarkable pairing of historical newsreel and contemporary television footage, a shot of the cheering crowds that greet the cavalcade of what appears to be a Nazi parade offers an especially uncanny experience when graphically matched with a shot of bike riders and cheering crowds at the Tour de France cycling event. With regard to Godard's framing of historical memory, it is notable that the latter shot shows a bike rider whose shirt-emblazoned team sponsor, the Spanish telecommunications company Movistar, becomes a linguistic variation on the term movie star. At the same time, in each of these shots (of a Nazi parade and the Tour de France), the crowd-lined roads, with people cheering and waving (including, in the first instance, the Nazi salute) and the vehicles that move along the depth-axis of the 3D image (from background to foreground and foreground to background, respectively), assume an altogether different quality when their inherent depth is brought into new focus and historical perspective by the contemporary 3D context.

In a rare instance of excerpted footage from a film that is itself 3D in native form, there is even a playful reference – repeated across *Goodbye to Language* and *The Three Disasters* – to *Piranha 3D* (Alexandre Aja, 2010), in which a bloodied, drowning woman splashes in and out of the water – oscillating in her throes between movements towards the foreground and background of the frame – as she is pulled by a boat in whose motor her hair is trapped. In its relocated cultural context, this footage functions as an ironic comment on the sensational role that 3D cinema has traditionally served in the film industry, whether as novelty and spectacle in the 1950s or in the post-*Avatar* (James

Figures 5.7–5.8 Footage of a Nazi parade (top) and the Tour de France (bottom) as represented in *Goodbye to Language*

Cameron, 2009) boom in commercial 3D filmmaking of recent years, to which *Goodbye to Language* and *The Three Disasters* arguably respond.

In another 3D film, *Final Destination 5* (Steven Quale, 2011), excerpted in *The Three Disasters*, the 3D-ness of the image, a marketable spectacle in its original context, is foregrounded to the point of reflexive distanciation, with the 3D effect almost entirely shorn of narrative context, consciously eschewing the typical strategies of an industrial 3D cinema. The film is characterised generally by what Miriam Ross describes as 'the avoidance of so-called gimmick shots in which objects seem to fly towards viewers' (Ross 2016). In this instance, however, isolating precisely the gimmick, a woman is seen falling from a great height, plunging towards a sailboat directly below her, all the while filmed from above, before her torso is skewered by the boat's mast, which, in turn, protrudes through and beyond her prone body, emerging towards the screen, extending as if directly towards the spectator. Godard exploits what would be anathema to industrial 3D cinema, abstracting an already self-conscious play with 3D representation into pure movement or form, liberating the image from its narrative and industrial dimensional contexts.

Elsewhere in *The Three Disasters*, another editing technique is used to create an alternative hybrid of 3D imagery constructed from 2D sources. Reworking his earlier *(Hi)story(ies) of Cinema*, Godard uses excerpts of superimpositions of archival 2D film images, one layered atop the other, to create a further hybrid 3D effect, somewhere between the flat or planar image of its 2D originals and the full 3D effect of natively rendered or in-camera stereoscopy – in this respect, perhaps a cinephilic variation on the industrial trend to create the 3D effect retrospectively in post-production, rather than natively or in-camera. In one instance, which uses imagery from F. W. Murnau's *Nosferatu: A Symphony of Horror* (*Nosferatu. Eine Symphonie des Grauens*, 1922), the eponymous vampire of Murnau's silent original haunts the 3D present, too, when layered atop another film entirely. Claws outstretched in vampiric pose, cloak aloft, the shadow of the vampire's outstretched arms envelops a crowd of laughing theatre-goers when superimposed over footage of a vaudeville audience from King Vidor's *The Crowd* (1928). The vampirism is implied by the depth dimension of the composite image and the relations between its constituent elements – first 2D (in each film's original context), then 2D layered on top of 2D (in their reworking within *(Hi)story(ies) of Cinema*) and finally in 3D as this intermediary work is further referenced in *The Three Disasters*. Such densely reflexive, visually complex montages of archival sources is not new to Godard, as *(Hi)story(ies) of Cinema* reminds us. What is new is the means to create implied three-dimensional relations in this footage, for example, as keyed in via the visual effects software that allows for 3D separation in footage not produced in the stereoscopic parallel of paired left-eye and right-eye cameras.

In a corollary of the focus on the stereoscopic image, the sounds of archival sources are also processed in order to examine stereophonic and monophonic (or monaural) sound within a historical framework. Such sound–image relations evidence the degree to which, as Albertine Fox has written, Godard is concerned with 'thinking historically about 3D filmmaking practice' (Fox 2018: 184). As she suggests of *Goodbye to Language*, but with equal relevance to *The Three Disasters*, a Godard film 'cannot be treated as a solitary art work but it must be heard through its correspon-

dences with other films and documents' (Fox 2018: 181), including specifically the 'manipulation of the acoustics, colouring and textures in *Adieu
au langage* [*Goodbye to Language*], whose abstract, sensuous and painterly
qualities are extended by way of the 3D effect' (Fox 2018: 184). As with
Godard's broader sound scheme, the stereo properties of sound mixing are
utilised in order to systematically subvert a conventional sound mix. This
includes what Fox terms 'a succession of tactile audio-visual harmonies'
(Fox 2018: 190) through which

> the spectator's relationship with the sounds and pictures is misaligned
> and realigned as Godard persistently searches for different ways to
> forge new radical associations and make sounds and images heard in
> all their opacity, with a kinetic intensity that causes our ears to ring.
> (Fox 2018: 191)

Notably, such ringing might occur in one or both ears simultaneously. That
is, soundtracks are referenced or sampled in ways that both memorialise and
remix, emphasising stereo sound and separation even in the instance of films not
originally intended for stereo playback. In *The Three Disasters*, for example, the
theme, sung by Peggy Lee for Nicholas Ray's *Johnny Guitar* (1954), is played
over images of another Ray film, *They Live by Night* (1948). In this overdubbed
soundtrack, we hear the plaintive lyrics from *Johnny Guitar* – 'Whether you
go, whether I stay, I love you' – as a substitute for *They Live by Night*, whose
soundtrack is absent but whose image track we see, as a character delivers her
own expression of tortured love – also 'I love you' – words written by her now
slain outlaw lover. Not only is the original's soundtrack replaced, rendering image
track and soundtrack misaligned, in Fox's terms, but this alternative soundtrack
is further remixed, with the stereo field moving variously from the left ear to
the right ear and back again, seemingly without clear motivation, as the original
mono soundtrack is output variably through left and/or right channels.

Similar anti-classical strategies are evident in countless Godard films, but
what is distinctive in the 3D cinematic context is how this experimentation
with sound functions in parallel with the director's approach to the image
track. That is, this play with sound offers a stereophonic variation on the
simultaneous construction and deconstruction of stereoscopic imaging by way
of underlying left-eye and right-eye images as well as left-ear and right-ear
sounds, which are in conflict in *Goodbye to Language* and *The Three Disasters*
on numerous occasions.

Here and elsewhere, the 3D context and linguistic framing of *Goodbye to
Language* and *The Three Disasters* suggest something other than simple archival
commemoration. Instead, these films exist within the creative realm of a technologically mediated film historiography, rooted in an attempt to interrogate

the representational dynamics of 3D cinema, as placed within historical context. Reflexively looking both backwards and forwards, *Goodbye to Language* and *The Three Disasters* move fluidly from 3D to 2D – as well as stereo to mono – and back again, charting historical and dimensional relations that are implicitly and explicitly brought into relief by Godard's comparative dialectics.

Intertextual Vectors of Love and Death

If, in *Goodbye to Language* and *The Three Disasters*, the intercutting of archival footage with contemporary scenes shot for 3D encourages a comparative reading, archival moving images are also located within the space of the diegesis itself. In these instances, cine-historical relations are drawn *within* rather than *between* individual shots and through an intertextual mise-en-scène (and its 3D rendering) rather than editing. In Godard's positioning of 2D images within the 3D optical field, there is a further cinephilic conjuring of the history and historical memory of cinema through stereoscopic spectres rendered in the form of intertextual vectors of love and death. These come to the viewer in a spatial reimagining that sees the cumulative and evolving history of cinematic images (a temporal axis) mapped perspectivally in 3D (a spatial axis). Whether the spectator extends towards these archival images through a process of immersion, or whether these natively 2D images extend towards the spectator through a process of emergence, the z-dimension becomes the principal axis for Godard's 3D historiography of the cinematic image and its inscribed technologies of representation.

On several occasions, especially in *Goodbye to Language*, footage from the past is shown in motion on a large television set located within the film's newly shot scenes, with the plane of the 2D image situated within spaces visually represented in 3D. This televisually and then cinematically mediated footage features several films, including Rouben Mamoulian's *Dr. Jekyll and Mr. Hyde* (1931), Henry King's *The Snows of Kilimanjaro* (1952), Boris Barnet's *By the Bluest of Seas* (*U samogo sinego morya*, 1936) and Fritz Lang's *Metropolis* (1927). For Scott, such scenes investigate 'paradoxes of flatness and depth, for example, the way the flat surface of a television showing an old-fashioned two-dimensional movie changes the volume of a room' (Scott 2014: 5). Yet, in the paradoxes that Scott refers to, in addition to a consideration of volume, there is also a historiographic dialogue – the 2D image and the flatness of the televisual screen, in comparison with its spatialisation within the mise-en-scène and its subsequent positioning within the depth of field of 3D cinematic representation.

In the instance of *Dr. Jekyll and Mr. Hyde*, female characters (one from *Dr. Jekyll and Mr. Hyde*, the other from *Goodbye to Language*), each semi-naked and clinging to a drape, are graphically matched within the same frame – that is, the contemporary frame that encompasses the frame within the frame of

Figure 5.9 Spatial relations and the televisual playback of *Dr. Jekyll and Mr. Hyde* in *Goodbye to Language*

Dr. Jekyll and Mr. Hyde in televisual playback in *Goodbye to Language*. In further shots, this spatially mediated relationship between these women (one via a television screen, the other in the wider mise-en-scène) as represented in *Goodbye to Language* is drawn not only through the graphical symmetry of the left and right of the frame in balanced composition, but a symmetry structured in terms of depth, too, by way of a centrally positioned male character in Godard's fiction, who forms a triangular meeting point – most explicit when rendered in 3D – for these twinned female figures. The z-dimensional axis connects bodies and texts alike across Godard's and Mamoulian's fictions of narrative and formal doubling, for which the double life of Jekyll/Hyde is an apt allusion.

Similarly, with regard to *The Snows of Kilimanjaro*, a character in conversation is partly mirrored by Godard's own character in *Goodbye to Language*, who dresses in front of a bright light, backlit to an extreme, with the lamp causing optical lens flare throughout the duration of the shot. This underlying light source becomes playfully doubled, the source of the projected illumination ambiguous, when the characters of *The Snows of Kilimanjaro* strike a match that now appears, as if by trans-historical and extra- or intertextual illusion as well as allusion, to be a source of the lens flare that hovers in the foreground of the 3D frame.

In *Goodbye to Language*, referencing *Metropolis* as a further variation, a female figure in Lang's film is pictured in slow motion on the television screen as Godard's own female character is pictured alongside and to the fore of this screen. The two bodies are spatially depicted in implied relations through an effect of depth that connects figures and planes. These bodies – in a choreography that spans decades, films, fictions and technologies – move in parallel in a number of ways. At times they appear to mirror one another, at other times they appear to interact with one another, in all instances via a perspectival, spatial illusion. In one example, the directional gaze of the character in *Metropolis*, directed off-screen in its original context, is now relocated by a television screen within the larger mise-en-scène. The gaze is met by the corresponding gaze, in eye-line match, of the now-twinned female character of *Goodbye to Language*.

The referencing of *By the Bluest of Seas* offers a further variation on this use of the television within the mise-en-scène of *Goodbye to Language* to create a dimensionally articulated dialogue with film history. A scene from *By the Bluest of Seas* plays back on the television screen within the space of *Goodbye to Language*. It is intercut with what appears to be an extra-diegetic excerpt from the same film. However, the referentiality of this sequence is rendered somewhat ambiguously. Although it appears to be an extra-diegetic excerpt, it might not be. Rather, the particular quality and grainy texture of this footage, as well as what appears to be the occasional reflection of light off a screen, suggests that it may in fact have been filmed directly from the television screen itself, which further complicates its technological mediation and historical relations. In this representation of *By the Bluest of Seas*, the filmic reference shifts temporal registers as well as visual perspectives.

As a final excerpted shot of *By the Bluest of Seas* plays back on the television screen within the mise-en-scène, a further choreographed doubling of bodies occurs. In Godard's contemporary fiction, a male character drapes himself over the legs of his female companion, a grasping, near-prostrate figure who graphically matches a preceding televisually mediated image of a shipwrecked figure who washes ashore in *By the Bluest of Seas*. Again, 2D images from the past and their contemporary 3D variants are placed in dialogue along the spatial axis of the 3D image.

That these film images are represented on a television screen is also significant to the spatial, dimensional and perspectival historiography of *Goodbye to Language* and *The Three Disasters*. After all, different screens necessarily carry different signification, and the cinematic image assumes a particular resonance when visualised apart from its historical context of theatrical projection, especially when a 2D source is subsequently rendered in the mise-en-scène of a 3D film.

On two occasions, there are even shots of the visual noise of a television screen, which is turned on without a signal. It, too, becomes a source of visual interest in this 3D representation of the markers or traces of media technology. Moreover, depending on the specific conditions of our own viewing, the televisual mediation of filmic images might even be a source of comparison – of images, technologies and modes of spectatorship. In this regard, the role of the television as a site of mediation within *Goodbye to Language* will inevitably take on different meaning if Godard's films are being experienced in the home via 3D-capable equivalents of the television screen on which existing films are represented within the mise-en-scène of *Goodbye to Language* and *The Three Disasters*.

As Francesco Casetti has argued, there is a particular meaning in the rupture, tension or disjuncture that comes when what he describes as 'poor images' circulate within an otherwise overwhelmingly high-tech context, such as 3D:

> If the recourse to high definition – and in particular to 3-D – permitted cinema to give spectators the world represented in such a way that they could literally feel it at their fingertips, then this embrace of low definition – with images taken from security systems, hand-held cameras, smartphones, the Internet, and the like – serves to wake up these same spectators, to alert them, to make them reflect on what it means to represent the world today. (Casetti 2015: 119)

For Godard, in one such reflexive endeavour, there is a tension between high and low resolution, including as an element of medium-specific noise. The so-called poor image – to which we might add the poor sound – assumes new meaning when situated within otherwise high-tech or high-def contexts, to the extent that, as Casetti notes, '[t]he adoption of poor images allows for the opening of a different space in which to maneuver' (Casetti 2015: 118). Godard's 3D cinema might be thought of as one such manoeuvring, the opening of a different space – in this instance, dimensionally mapped – that is literal as well as figurative.

In all of these instances, particular meaning comes from the relocation of 2D images within a 3D context, and also from the particularities of relocating film-historical images within a contemporary technological-aesthetic milieu. For Ross, describing a dynamic of exchange rather than teleological or linear evolution, the radicalness of these encounters 'does not erase the significance of the older 2D footage but instead asks us to feel our way around the scenes' different visualscapes' (Ross 2016), with an emphasis on the processes of comparison and historical awareness. In these acts of 3D reframing as a way of engaging the cinematic past, film history is given new life, animated – or reanimated – via a reconfigured 3D gaze, returned to not as a relic or curio but as an intertextual vector in a cinematic – and, indeed, cinephilic – historiography, in which the 2D image and 3D image necessarily coexist.

CONCLUSION

In both *Goodbye to Language* and *The Three Disasters*, comparative imaging across technologies exists as a mode of reflexive historiography. For Raymond Bellour, referencing Daney, 'Godard, the strictly contemporary filmmaker "dedicated to the present" [. . .] continually positions himself in relation to cinema's past' (Bellour 1992: 217), adding that 'Godard tackles these old cinematic forms in a way that preserves what they express: both the old (cinema as it's always been done), and the new (the future of their own transformation)' (Bellour 1992: 217). Writing fifteen years later, Bellour describes Godard as a filmmaker who turns the present 'into both a prophetic anticipation and a nostalgic reinterpretation' (Bellour 2007: 11). This is a variation on Godard's own reflections on 'the archeology of film and the memory of a century' (Godard and Ishaghpour 2005 [2000]), which is crystallised in the revealing historiographic couplet, 'the urgency of the present/the redemption of the past' (Godard and Ishaghpour 2005 [2000]: 19–21). Grounded in a redemptive concern with film history – on its x-, y- and z- dimensions – images from the past constitute a significant part of Godard's concurrent investigation of contemporary cinematic forms in a reciprocal exchange that occurs along the depth-axis of 3D imaging.

In Godard's dialectical or doubly tensed engagement with 3D cinema and in the manifold meanings of his cinematic *adieu*, *Goodbye to Language* and *The Three Disasters* pivot between 2D and 3D, past and present, *adieu* as goodbye and *adieu* as hello, and, by extension, the death of cinema and its potential resurrection. Cinema itself – at least, in its present (or recently past) form – is one of those things to which Godard appears to be bidding *adieu*. Indeed, inasmuch as *Goodbye to Language* and – to a lesser extent – *The Three Disasters* present underlying narratives, these films are also about the technology and aesthetics of 3D imaging, as well as the history of film more generally. This is a history that is literally reframed; refiguring the technology and aesthetics of 3D cinema allows us to see anew the history of cinema as a medium, including via a spatialised historiography of perspectival relations amplified and emphasised in 3D. At the same time, this is also a history reframed symbolically in terms of the ways in which contemporary 3D cinema exists in the context of the 2D as well as 3D cinema that preceded it. Godard redefines our understanding of cinema as considered within a technological and historiographic framework that dynamically negotiates past and present. This moves both forwards and backwards in time and via the foreground and background of the frame as the history of cinema, and our historical memory of cinema, are delineated in three dimensions.

In reminding us of what is past (or passing), *Goodbye to Language* and *The Three Disasters* extend the laments, memorials and elegies of previous late-Godard films. Yet this process now also encompasses the transformative repercussions of the hardware and software of 3D cinema. *Goodbye to Language* and *The Three Disasters* articulate a departure – the former's *adieu* – consistent with the director's broader concern with the death of the medium in combination with the restless search for its reinvention – potentially contradictory notions that are nevertheless intimately intertwined in *Goodbye to Language* and *The Three Disasters*, to the point of being inseparable. In their stereoscopic images, and in their stereophonic sounds, these 3D films represent the creative dynamic between death and rebirth in the artistic process, both for individual artists (that is, filmmakers) and for a medium (that is, cinema).

Ultimately, as a reflection on cinema, and on its capacity for regeneration or renewal, Godard's *adieu* is not only a goodbye or farewell, but an *adieu* in the Levinasian sense of a double or multiple meaning. Specifically, it suggests the continued existence of cinema, for Godard, in the potential for ocular revisioning or linguistic re-articulation, rooted at least in part in the creative potential of a reconfigured technological apparatus, including the 3D image. Put simply, and utilised as a broader historiographic model, it is only in our recurring goodbyes to cinema that we might envisage its continued vitality.

CHAPTER 6

Voyaging in Deep Time: *Voyage of Time: The IMAX Experience*

As previous chapters have sought to illustrate, the sounds and images of film history are remarkably resilient, adapting to the present as reconfigured and reframed. In this concluding chapter, this cinematic reimagining occurs not via the amplified depth dimension of 3D, as discussed in Chapter 5, but in the expanded frames and screens of IMAX and the associated historical flows of moving images across time and technology.

If, as this book argues, film history is to be considered in its continuing resonances, the moving image itself can sometimes reveal the ways in which we might chart this history. That is, cinema offers its own visions for how we might place the contemporary cinematic moment into broader context, from micro to macro, and towards what Siegfried Zielinski, among others, has described as 'deep time' (see Zielinski 2006 [2002]), referring to the vast timescales involved in phenomena generally imperceptible to human senses and scales of experience and perception. This chapter maps the contours of one such expanded frame, analysing how Terrence Malick's *Voyage of Time* (2016), as an illustrative case study, engages theories of time and temporality, history and historicity, in relation to the past (or pasts) of cinema as it continues to reverberate in the present.

On the level of technology, the evolving cinematic apparatus offers a productive lens through which to reframe – both literally and figuratively – our understanding of cinema as a historical medium. Shifts in this apparatus – from imaging to exhibition – offer reconfigured means for addressing questions of history and historiography, with scientific notions of deep time and expanded temporality applied in the specific field of film history.

VOYAGE OF TIME: THE EXPANDED FRAMES OF IMAX

Considered in relation to conceptions of deep time – both that of the universe and that of cinema – and the visualisation or representation of these timespans, the documentary *Voyage of Time* – in its multiple versions, namely *Voyage of Time: The IMAX Experience*, *Voyage of Time: Life's Journey* and *Voyage of Time: The IMAX Experience in Ultra Widescreen 3.6*[1] – exists as a meditation on the changing technologies and aesthetics of cinema, including how we might historicise this medium on a micro- as well as a macro-historical scale.

Within the context of these parallel – and, in some ways, intersecting – temporal registers, *Voyage of Time* engages the history of the actual or literal universe but also the figurative universe of cinema's own tools, aesthetics and experiences. In its comparative imaging, spanning scientific as well as more recognisably cinematic practices of visualisation, *Voyage of Time* illuminates an expanded history of the moving image, connecting the cinematic to pre-, parallel and post-cinematic moments and modes. Likewise, the so-called premium large-format (PLF) screen on which *Voyage of Time* is exhibited suggests a formal and aesthetic corollary between an expanded frame (literally, in terms of the 70mm film frame and large-format screen of IMAX projection, including in Ultra Widescreen 3.6 variation) and an expanded historical framework (a macro-historical representation of the birth and death of the cosmos that might also be extrapolated as a reflection on the history of cinema itself).

The result is a film that illustrates, in its own thematic and representational concerns, the notion of deep time in particular, and scientific models of evolutionary history more generally – both in terms of how cinema might represent such temporal spans and how we might approach the moving image in its past, present and future iterations. *Voyage of Time* both directly engages the notion of deep time in geological terms, and indirectly engages the histories of cinematic representation, with an emphasis on the technologies and techniques of visualisation across science and cinema. Put another way, cosmic-planetary and media archaeological conceptions of time are intertwined in Malick's multi-screen explorations of the means of visualising universal history via the moving image.

The deep temporal concerns of this chapter are thus threefold: In the first instance, the deep time of the universe itself, generally estimated by scientists to be approximately 13.8 billion years.[2] In the second instance, the deep time of cinema, in terms of how the history of the cosmos might be rendered, formally and stylistically, as cinematic time. And in the third instance, a more abstract or theoretical understanding of deep time, with regard to the evolutionary history of cinema itself. Considered in a media archaeological context, the contours of the frame and screen might be thought of as analogous markers of the deep time that is depicted *on* that screen or screens. There is a double meaning, then, in the idea of an expanded frame – metaphorical or universal on the one hand, literal and rooted in the materiality of scientific and cinematic apparatuses on the other.

How, we might ask, does *Voyage of Time* encourage us to think differently about the history (or histories) of cinema? In what ways does its visualisation of cosmological deep time also function as a negotiation of historiographic discourses concerning cinema's own expanded history/histories? How, to switch registers, might an expanded temporal or historical frame illuminate the more literal frames (and their respective sites, screens and images) of cinema? What lessons might be gleaned from the discourses and practices of science with regard to history and time? And, ultimately, at what point in cinema's own evolutionary history – its voyage in time, if you will – do we find ourselves today?

Cosmic and Cinematic Temporalities

The whole history, not of this world alone, but of every sphere that is or has been, is still in vibrating existence, and one universal perception extending through the infinity would embrace within the tremblings of the boundless ether a consciousness of all that was or is, an eternal and universal living picture of all past events.
    – Henry V. Hopwood on the 'Past, Present, and Future' of cinema
(Hopwood 1899: 234)

The past. The present. The future. Experience the unfolding of time.
    – Official trailer for *Voyage of Time: The IMAX Experience* (2016)

As Hopwood reminds us – writing 117 years prior to Malick's universal history – cinema's own visions of light suggest certain affinities with the astral projections of universal time and related scientific histories, theories and imaginaries concerning, for example, the birth of the cosmos, the formation of geological matter and the evolution of the species.[3] Indeed, the science of the cosmos, and the scientific quest to perceive, understand and represent – visually or otherwise – the vast expanses that constitute universal history offer numerous models for how we might think about cinematic time and its history in relation to the finite and beyond – or, in Hopwood's terms, the past, present and future of the living picture.

Historically, the moving image has often functioned as a form of mediation, connecting scientific time to cinematic time (and vice versa) in visualising scientific practices and phenomena. From the earliest days of cinema, its ability to capture and manipulate time, to visualise scientific processes, brought filmmakers into dialogue with scientists. Films document and disseminate in many ways, including via the capacity of the cinematic apparatus to augment human perception, a key factor in its ability to represent temporal spans that might otherwise escape human perception. Accordingly, as Scott Curtis writes, scientific films, of one kind or another, are 'not rare' (Curtis 2013: 46). Literally thousands of 'researchers over the course of the last century used moving images in their work' (Curtis 2013: 46). This is because the development of cinema 'focused on temporal continuity (movement, growth)' (Curtis 2013: 50), as opposed to the discontinuity in representational methods 'up [to] this point (e.g., sequential slides, illustrations of stages of development, still photographs)' (Curtis 2013: 50).

In *Voyage of Time*, connections between cosmic and cinematic time are rendered literal, most obviously, in Malick's explicit attempt to represent the history of the cosmos, translating cosmic time (and the scientific theories and discourses thereof) into cinematic time (and the attendant cinematic theories and discourses), implicating the larger – or deeper – history of the various imaging technologies, lens-based and otherwise, which constitute both scientific and cinematic apparatuses.

Indeed, *Voyage of Time* seeks to represent nothing less than the entire history of the universe – framed as the story of time – in the span of mere minutes, as translated into cinema's own temporalities. A marketing tagline for the film invites the spectator to '[e]xperience the unfolding of time', linking the abstract and experiential in terms of our perception, via cinema, of temporal scales. In its depiction of evolutionary history, as one such unfolding, this temporal journey comprises the condensation of approximately 14 billion years: from the emergence of matter (and thus time) to its ultimate obsolescence. In broadly linear chronology, the film moves from the origins of the universe to the geological formation of the earth and the emergence of life through the Precambrian and Paleozoic to the current Anthropocene. Shifting tenses, beyond this present, *Voyage of Time* also speculatively depicts the demise of the planet in a distant future that sees the extinction of all the planet's species and the consumption of the earth by the sun – a history charted on the ultimate scale of a universal past, present and future.

The timescales represented by Malick's voyage are vast indeed. For example, within its billions of years of history: approximately 4.5 billion years ago, the earth was formed; approximately 3.5 billion years ago, the first forms of life appeared on earth in the shape of unicellular organisms; approximately 230 million years ago, the first dinosaurs appeared, only to be rendered extinct some 164 million years later; approximately 300,000 years ago, the first *Homo sapiens* appeared; and occurring in an unknown number of years into the future, the predicted end of the earth and, in turn, the universe.

In the domain of science – including science as represented by Malick – conceptualisations of immense periods of time necessarily abound; they are central to the fields of astrophysics, geology and biology, among others. The specific notion of deep time engages the most macro of scales. In scientific contexts, deep time typically refers to the multi-million- or even multi-billion-year spans associated with cosmological and other natural phenomena. Writing in 1981, for example, describing the 'basin and range' of ancient geological forms, John McPhee first used the term deep time to describe the vast timescales involved in the earth becoming the earth. A reconfigured temporal/historical scale was required, he argued, because of the difficulty in perceiving – let alone comprehending – such immense spans. As McPhee puts it, in attempting to communicate the ages, epochs, periods, eras, eons and supereons at the core of geological time, '[n]umbers do not seem to work well with regard to deep time. Any number above a couple of thousand years – fifty thousand, fifty million – will with nearly equal effect awe the imagination to the point of paralysis' (McPhee 1981: 20).

Nevertheless, if engaging with the awed imagination poses particular challenges, it also offers opportunities for greater historical awareness and historiographic reflection, including as applied to cinema – albeit on a considerably reduced temporal scale. Most obviously, science shares with cinema the use of the moving image for the purpose of observing, illustrating and visually (as well as sonically) representing temporal phenomena, cosmic and otherwise. Scientific discourses in general, and those pertaining to practices of scientific visualisation in particular, can be usefully applied outside of their original contexts, not least in terms of what Curtis describes as 'important historiographic questions and challenges to our discipline' (Curtis 2013: 46). The very issue of the methods, models, metaphors and means we use to make sense of significant historical spans – cosmic or cinematic – is arguably one such question and challenge.

Specifically, if dealing with such scales is routine in certain areas of science, in which millions of years exist as a blip, what of cinema and its own macrohistorical scales? The concept of deep time can also be applied to a variety of media, as is apparent in the field of media archaeology, concerned with periods of time greater than that of any one particular technical apparatus or configuration, let alone medium (see, for example, Parikka 2015; Zielinski 2006 [2002]). Instead, the emphasis is on 'technical media' (Zielinski 2006 [2002]) as constituted within the overarching historical endeavour of a broader history of audio-visuality – one that includes but is not limited to that of cinema.

In *Voyage of Time*, bridging representational and historiographic concerns, voiceover narration outlines a central focus on deep time and the evolution of the universe in cinematic distillation. 'Why did dust become life?' asks the narrator of *Voyage of Time: The IMAX Experience*, explicitly framing these temporal thematics. 'Why was there something before nothing?'

When it comes to representing these enigmatic enquiries, if countless theorists have pondered the particularities of cinematic time and the translation of external realities into the medium and language of film, the case of deep time is distinct in a number of respects. A. O. Scott proclaims Malick as 'one of modern cinema's great masters of distended and compacted chronology' (Scott 2016: 9), and an authorial reading of *Voyage of Time* might point to thematic and other continuities with what James Batcho describes as Malick's cinema of 'a temporal shift' (see Batcho 2018: 115–54). Ultimately, the very question of the representability (or otherwise) of deep time raises particular issues.

Across fields, for example, the challenge of deep temporal representation, especially addressing the history of the universe, is inextricably connected with science and its own histories of observation and representation and the specific practices of scientific visualisation. Attempts to register such spans necessarily involve scales of translation that are difficult even to comprehend, let alone represent. 'Condensing billions and billions and billions of years into a 45-minute film is a tall order', writes Erin Wayman (2016: 29), identifying this very problem. Even the *Voyage of Time* production notes acknowledge this complexity, noting how

> Malick's film traverses deep swaths of time – the yardstick of geologists, yet one that can disorient human minds and derail the natural compression of storytelling. Geologists [. . .] are able to do a kind of 'mental gymnastics' to grasp talking about, say, a million years as a brief blip, but human brains aren't well-suited to contemplating that kind of epic scale.

While human beings may not be equipped to perform such mental gymnastics, what *cinematic* gymnastics could be performed in a film?

As a time-based medium, cinema has always held the capacity to temporally compress (or expand) in order to illustrate a range of scientific processes. In *Voyage of Time*, cosmic time is represented as cinematic time via a series of processes of downconversion or transnumeration, which abridge this massive universal history into the duration of a typical film – in this instance, less than an hour in its IMAX versions and approximately an hour-and-a-half in its non-IMAX version.

In seeking to represent universal history and render it visible to the human eye, the necessary mediation between scientific and cinematic discourses and apparatuses is not simply a matter of mathematical formulae – a numerical calculation. Rather, it entails the technological and aesthetic processes of cinematic representation, mediated in turn by way of the imaging properties of a range of technologies – from the specific tools and techniques of imaging to the particularities of the so-called cinematic experience – each replete with their own inherent temporalities and inscribed histories and historicity. Put another way, this is not simply the empirical equation of a ratio (something like 163,520,000,000,000:1 if we take the approximately 45 minutes of *Voyage of Time: The IMAX Experience* as our measure in relation to the no less than approximately 14 billion years of history it depicts). What makes this analysis more complex is that cinematic representation necessarily also involves its own contingencies of time and scale. *Voyage of Time* illustrates relationships between commensurate and incommensurate scales and measures of time – including in the translations and transpositions of its various technologies and techniques of visualisation.

A Voyage of Visuality

In articulating its titular journey, *Voyage of Time* also constitutes a voyage of visuality of sorts – in this instance, in the specific quest to represent or visualise the deep time of the universe. In such a reading, emphasis is on the historical as well as contemporary confluences of the practices of scientific visualisation and cinematic representation, which might be considered as inscriptions of an archaeology of the technological in an evolving history of the moving image.

In the realm of science, in representing cosmic phenomena, scientific visualisation has historically sought to translate deep temporal spans into frameworks or registers of human perception, an act of scaling that pushes at the extremes of representation. From the microscope to the telescope and countless technologies beyond, science has sought to extend the range of this perception, both empirically and speculatively.

Necessarily, since the temporal concerns of *Voyage of Time* both pre- and postdate the existence of the earth and depict a series of events that occurred millennia before the era of humans, *Voyage of Time* encompasses a range of different practices, combining extant scientific visualisations alongside more traditional modes of cinematic representation, including CGI and other visual effects. Certain phenomena are newly photographed by Malick: shots of boiling lava and volcanic magma demonstrate how the *terra firma* of the earth was formed, for example, while actors portray the life of *Homo erectus*. Other imagery is sourced from scientific laboratories, combining a range of observational tools. Still other images are variously visualised, in the scientific sense of the word – that is, modelled, animated, simulated or otherwise rendered: from an artistic impression of the formation of a membrane, the suspected source of the first life on earth, to computer simulations and other modelling of astronomical phenomena and events, such as the so-called Big Bang, for which no photographic images do or could exist.

In addition to the elisions of hard cuts that span, suture and thus elide millions or billions of years in a single edit, we witness few if any of the more familiar cinematic tropes of temporal compression (time-lapse photography, the speeding up of motion and so on). Instead, we see a translation via the fundamental formal properties of cinematic imaging – and, in turn, exhibition. A number of technologies and techniques engage the scientific quest to observe and document the universe, with lens-based and other visualisations of science recontextualised as represented by cinema.

Most explicitly, alongside newly shot footage, a series of extant scientific visualisations and other images are adopted and augmented. Malick uses material depicting the vast scale of the cosmos, including footage of black holes and other dark matter, the early stages of a supernova and the solar energies of light and heat emitted by the sun.

One such visualisation uses scientific data to illustrate what happens inside a black hole, an area of space that cannot be photographed – as the term implies – because it emits or reflects no light.[4] Black holes are otherwise detected and visualised by way of their interactions with surrounding matter. This is the case with the imagery contained in *Voyage of Time*, which shows a ring of gas and other matter as it is pulled into orbit around a black hole and as the overwhelming effects of gravity bend and distort space–time.

In another instance of a simulation that seeks to visualise a deep temporal phenomenon, *Voyage of Time* includes footage that simulates the formation of galaxies, potentially over billions of years.[5] In terms of scale, this period reveals the ways in which galaxies evolve over time, with particular focus on the presence of hydrogen gas. Hydrogen is a key element in star formation and its visualisation is thus a means for scientists to measure and illustrate galactic evolution. Because hydrogen is especially difficult to observe, a computer-modelled simulation – that is, one derived from mathematical data – allows the visualisation of an otherwise unrepresentable phenomenon, across a timescale that equally exceeds both human perception and photographic representation.

Elsewhere still, a further simulation depicts the collision of two galaxies.[6] When galaxies collide – a scenario that may occur with our own galaxy[7] – they either merge into a single galaxy or continue their respective journeys in space. Again, scientific visualisation represents the course of billions of years in a matter of seconds or minutes.

In other examples, to shift technologies as well as ontologies, astronomical imagery is derived from the light directly observed during scientific observations as sourced via telescopes of one kind or another. Imagery of the Cigar Galaxy (aka Messier 82 or NGC 3034), which depicts the elliptical shape of this starburst galaxy as gaseous clouds that extend from its centre, is sourced from observed light via the National Aeronautics and Space Administration (NASA) Hubble Space Telescope.[8] Other sources of imagery include NASA's Solar Dynamics Observatory,[9] a satellite equipped to permanently observe the activities of the sun, footage from which is utilised in *Voyage of Time* to depict coronal eruptions and other solar activity.

Alongside data visualisations and images of directly observable phenomena, *Voyage of Time* also evidences a range of hybrid and augmented imaging practices. For example, visualisations and newly photographed images are integrated with a variety of visual effects. Numerous scenes include artistic interpretations of one kind or another, rooted, to a greater or lesser degree, in scientific data. Such visual effects, writes Wayman, 'bring to life the formation of the planets, the origin of the first cells, the demise of the sun and other events that scientists can only imagine' (Wayman 2016: 29). Here and elsewhere, artistic or speculative renderings are used to represent a range of such phenomena.

Figures 6.1–6.2 Scientific simulations of a black hole (top) and galaxy formation (bottom) as represented in *Voyage of Time: The IMAX Experience*

In one example, CGI is used to depict the Jurassic and Cretaceous periods, including Muttaburrasaurus dinosaurs, and subsequently the Cretaceous–Paleogene (K–Pg) meteor event (circa approximately 66 million years ago) that led to the extinction of the dinosaurs.

At other times, further complicating the ontologies of the film's visual effects, images that might have been generated digitally are instead depicted using a variety of analogue photographic techniques. In order to approximate certain scientific phenomena, for example, Malick employed what the film's production notes describe as chemical experiments with 'various liquids, dyes,

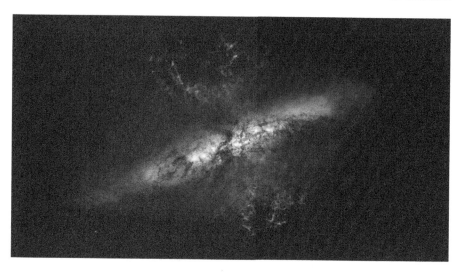

Figure 6.3 A Hubble Space Telescope image as represented in *Voyage of Time: The IMAX Experience*

gasses and fluids' (2016), filming these substances and materials in various states of suspension. The result is a series of abstract images that represent scientific phenomena that might otherwise exceed either direct photographic reproduction or the visualisation of empirical data.

With regard to other imaging devices, in the context of comparative imaging across fields, laboratory-sourced visualisations are also combined with more ostensibly cinematic methods and tools. These include the use of 65mm cameras specific to the IMAX format, which are designed to ensure images of an especially high resolution.

At the same time, *Voyage of Time* also punctuates this high-tech imagery – whether its scientific visualisations or the industrial cinematography of IMAX-specific 65mm cameras – with footage shot using the decidedly low-tech or consumer-tech iPhone-like Digital Harinezumi portable camera. The Harinezumi, like other contemporary consumer digital imaging devices, is a hand-held, battery-powered camera capable of filming still and moving images. Here, its footage, shot in multiple geographical locations (a parallel to the film's more pointedly geological planetary concerns), is inserted into an otherwise ostensibly linear evolutionary history. If there are other formal and thematic reasons for such a choice, the result is also a comparative or reflexive approach to the contemporary proliferation of such devices and their aesthetic inscription. The additional complexities – in terms of scale and scope – of how these assorted devices/images are subsequently relocated and reframed include the specific exhibition context of IMAX.

At times, it is not always clear where one source ends and the next begins, blurring the boundaries between photography and cinematography, visualisation and visual effects and science and cinema. The technologies used, and the underlying ontologies of their methods of representation, are frequently hybrid. Specifically, images – including those sourced from research laboratories and other scientific institutions – are altered or augmented in a variety of ways. In representing European Southern Observatory (ESO) imagery of the Milky Way's Orion constellation reflection nebula (aka Messier 78 or NGC 2068),[10] for example, Malick overlays nebulous gases and other elements in order to create an image that is more detailed than the original, even at the risk of compromising the accuracy of his representations. In other shots, CGI is integrated with photographic material, in a mix of scientific visualisation and artistic rendering, combining photographic, scientific-simulatory and other, hybrid ontologies. As one example, digital imaging is matted in a shot that depicts the scientifically predicted end of the earth. In it, the foreground appears to be a desert, yet one in which the sky above is meticulously painted in, using digital effects to animate an apocalyptic vision, with this composite of real landscapes and CGI details illustrating one possible scenario for the planet's end.

In all of these instances, in depicting celestial spectacles, geological events and biological phenomena, the representations of *Voyage of Time*, including its use of extant scientific visualisations, seek to translate the temporal expanses of the universe into a comprehensive visual language. In doing so, these are images that implicitly reveal a wider media history, even while representing the more explicit thematic concern with universal history. In translating these temporalities into the parallel realms of human perception and cinematic representation, this voyage of visuality across media is a reminder of cinema's own evolution, including its technologies of representation – and, as we shall see, its technologies of exhibition.

The Screen as Universe

Not all screens are equal, of course, and there are particularities in the precise context of the screen (or screens) on which the universe is depicted and in the broader exhibition conditions of this cosmic projection. This is especially the case in the extremes of microscopic and macroscopic representations, from the intracellular to the intergalactic. The scale and scope of the frame/screen itself is also implicated in these representations – from premium large-format IMAX to Ultra Widescreen 3.6, in the instance of *Voyage of Time*. The particular choice of IMAX – in 2016, for a film on this particular subject – might be explained in part by its long history in the fields of science and education in addition to its housing within museums and other institutions (see Griffiths 2008). Moreover, there is something distinctive in the formal properties of this

Figures 6.4–6.5 Enhanced or composite footage in *Voyage of Time: The IMAX Experience*, depicting a nebula (top) and desertscape (bottom)

format and its particular cinematic experience in relation to Malick's thematic concerns with the vastness of the universe and the scales of deep time. In a further cinematic reframing, the screen becomes the universe, and the universe becomes the screen, as scientific visualisations and other images are rescaled within the macroscopic-microscopic (and microscopic-macroscopic) contexts of the large-format frame and its dimensional relations.

IMAX has particular characteristics, both in relation to its own scale and scope and how, in the instance of *Voyage of Time*, underlying scientific visualisations are reconfigured in different iterations of the cinematic experience.

In its approximately fifty-year history, the IMAX format, marketed precisely in terms of its expanded image size, has lent itself to an exploration of scale, often foregrounded – implicitly or explicitly – in the subject matter of IMAX-specific films that can align form and content. As early as 1970, writing in *American Cinematographer*, one industry professional, Roman Kroiter, offered his own assessment, suggesting that

> when the public wants to go out to a movie, it better be better. Technically it will have to be eyeball-filling high-fidelity. Artistically it will have to be breaking through new frontiers, not the millionth re-hash of the same old cliches. The world isn't going to stand still, and the movies won't either. Things are going to change. (Kroiter 1970: 799)

The precise definition of change may mean many different things, of course, though an eyeball-filling experience, as one facet of such large-format cinema, was already foregrounded in 1970, in the industrial discourses surrounding this system.

With respect to the frontier that constitutes the bounds of the frame itself, as well as the screen onto which its image is projected, the tri-version/tri-format release strategy of *Voyage of Time* warrants further examination. *Voyage of Time* is an exception to the overwhelming majority of the forty-two films released in IMAX and other premium large-format screens in the United States in 2016,[11] for which the IMAX site is effectively a secondary market for the further distribution of a film essentially identical across versions in all but screen size. In contrast, *Voyage of Time* is markedly different in its respective versions for IMAX and non-IMAX sites. When considered in comparative analysis, these discrete versions – across IMAX, IMAX Ultra Widescreen 3.6 and traditional theatrical releases – illustrate distinct screen architectures as well as certain properties of scale and scope in depicting the temporal (and spatial) expanses of the universe.

In terms of format, the film's versions span 35mm and 70mm film frames, as well as the IMAX Digital Format (IDF) and IMAX with Laser formats. In its IMAX-native footage, *Voyage of Time* was shot using 65mm film, which – along with other gauges from other devices – was then transferred to 70mm film (or its digital equivalent) for distribution in certain IMAX theatres and 35mm film (or its digital equivalent) for distribution in other sites. The difference in scale is significant: if one might imagine the 70mm frame to be precisely double the size of the 35mm frame, it is actually closer to a full nine times the size of a traditional 35mm image because the image is rotated on its side and printed vertically rather than horizontally within the frame, spanning multiple perforations.

In terms of aspect ratio, too, and a temporal–spatial translation that sees a thematic focus on deep time spatially translated into large formats and wide screens, the various versions of *Voyage of Time* range from the relatively conventional 1.85:1 of non-IMAX 35mm theatrical projection to the 3.6:1 aspect ratio of its Ultra Widescreen 3.6 limited IMAX release, as well as the more conventional aspect ratios (typically ranging from 1.43:1 to 1.9:1, depending on the exact theatre) of IMAX projection in its more familiar configurations.

Aligned to this scale is the absolute rather than relative size of the screen onto which each of these versions – and their respective film formats and aspect ratios – is projected. Within the site of the typical IMAX theatre, for example, such images span many tens of feet wide and many tens of feet high. Francesco Casetti writes of 'the large IMAX screen, which functions above all as an environment' (Casetti 2015: 57), wherein immersive images, he adds, 'aim at intensifying the level of the cinematographic experience through greater involvement of our senses' (Casetti 2015: 106). But which senses? And via which dimensions?

Across these dimensional expansions – height, width or both – of frame, screen and projected aspect ratio, a fundamental translation occurs in articulating the spans of the universe in temporal terms, via the contours of the cinematic image into spatial terms. The size of the frame and the size of the image offer their own spectacular appeal – a technological or cinematic-experiential sublime – but also function as a formal corollary of the vastness of the universe and its near 14-billion-year history. In short, there is a relationship between the scale of the universe and the scope of the IMAX screen, and, in the instance of Ultra Widescreen 3.6, that of its amplified aspect ratio. The contours of the frame/screen, and the distinctive dynamics of the cinematic experience, function in parallel with the cosmic phenomena depicted by *Voyage of Time* on the level of representation.

At one extreme, placing cosmic and other phenomena into focus, there is an emphasis in the film on microscopic and even subatomic levels. Connecting apparatuses across disciplines and centuries, imagery is derived from traditional microscopy, electron-microscopy and specialist macro-photographic techniques that capture and enlarge through dedicated lenses, framing tiny objects in extreme close-up, via an especially large reproduction ratio (that is, the ratio of the subject size as captured on the camera's film plane or sensor plane in relation to the subject's actual size).

Yet when represented via IMAX, the micro is also amplified in scale, beyond even the transformations of traditional cinematic representation, in a pairing of microscopic phenomena and macroscopic projection. To see images of microscopic matter (such as unicellular organisms) on a macro scale (in this instance, IMAX) creates a micro-macro/macro-micro disjuncture that is, in the purest sense of the term, spectacular. The centuries-old scientific pursuit of lens-based microscopy (circa approximately 400 years ago) as a means to visualise and document the otherwise imperceptible is here combined with the more recent cinematic phenomenon of the augmentation of ocular perception via the camera lens as a source of magnification and the further transformations in scale provided by cinema screens of greater and greater size. This combination of micro-macroscopic visualisation, the pairing of micro focus (in terms of subject matter) and macro scale (the 70mm film frame and IMAX screen), is used, for example, in numerous extreme close-ups of bacterial activity. At the other extreme, shifting from the microscopic to the macroscopic, the IMAX screen is also utilised as a means to represent the vastest expanses of the cosmos, including the particular reframing that comes via IMAX.

In *Voyage of Time*, this temporal–spatial translation is evident in computer-simulated footage that models dark matter, which constitutes some of the very largest structures in the universe, namely galaxies and galaxy clusters.[12] In temporal terms, the footage illustrates in the span of a matter of seconds the formation of cosmic structures over billions of years, as luminous nodes illustrate galactic activity via interconnected filaments in an otherwise empty expanse. Meanwhile, in spatial terms, this simulation models approximately 100 million light years in *distance*, a temporal–spatial span mapped in simulation within the geometric bounds of its framed visualisation. This is further represented – depending on the particular version of the film – across the 70mm image of the IMAX film strip and as projected at expanded scale on the IMAX screen.

Indeed, it is worth remembering that the dimensions of the cosmos, in terms of distance, are already mapped as a unit of time, commonly known as light years. These transposed discrete dimensions are further reconfigured in the course of scientific visualisation first, and cinematic representation second. In

Figure 6.6 One hundred million light years of spatialised time in a scientific visualisation as represented in *Voyage of Time: The IMAX Experience*

other words, *Voyage of Time* explicitly structures the temporal–spatial relationship as one of dimensional transposition not only at the level of science but also of cinema in which the fundamental architectures of the frame and screen are implicated and foregrounded. In aligning the *cosmic* universe and the *cinematic* universe, the representation of dark matter describes a vast expanse whose dimensions expand both the cosmos and the frame/screen.

The case of the Ultra Widescreen 3.6 version of *Voyage of Time* offers further illustration of this cosmic–cinematic corollary. It was distributed on the large-format screen of IMAX, but with the height of the frame constrained by the proportions of the horizontally elongated Ultra Widescreen image (effectively, the matting of top and bottom). If, as Ariel Rogers notes, '[t]he term *widescreen* generally refers to films with aspect ratios significantly greater than the pre-1953 Academy standard of 1.37:1 (usually reaching at least 1.66:1)' (Rogers 2013: 22), a 3.6:1 aspect ratio significantly exceeds these more typical dimensions in its proportional width. Dating back to the 1950s, widescreen formats have generally been marketed as offering 'a new form of cinematic experience' (Rogers 2013: 19), one rooted in 'the prospect of close, tactile contact with overwhelming images' (Rogers 2013: 20). In this instance, the Ultra Widescreen 3.6 version of *Voyage of Time* might also be read as a technologically mediated aligning of form and content.

In this respect, *Voyage of Time* also recalls what critics in the mid- to late 1960s and early 1970s called expanded cinema, which sought not only to experiment *within* the bounds of the frame and screen, but also to extend the size, type and number of frames/screens. This would enable a formal expansion into dimensions of time and space – and, indeed, perception and consciousness – otherwise constrained by the contours, ratios, dimensions and proportions of existing frame formats and screen sizes. For Gene Youngblood, writing in 1970, expanded cinema was concerned with the emerging 'image-making technologies that promise to extend man's communicative capacities beyond his most extravagant visions' (Youngblood 1970: 41). Such extravagant visions included those projected on the IMAX-precursor screens (the Multivision system that would later become known as IMAX) exhibited at Expo '70, at the same time that Youngblood wrote about expanded cinema. For Youngblood, this was 'a revolutionary projection system to be included in a chain of local theatres with screens seven stories high [. . .] a seven-storey image of perfect steadiness and crystal clarity' (Youngblood 1970: 352). Such a system, for Youngblood, promised the dual expansions – of inner and outer space, as mediated via a literally and figuratively expanded apparatus – that would encourage or reflect a similarly expanded consciousness.

Whether in these or other resonances, across a number of axes, and in the imaging and projection of both scientific and cinematic images, the particularities of IMAX – whether in Ultra Widescreen 3.6 or otherwise – extend the historical possibilities of deep temporal representation in both scientific visualisations and in their cinematic reframing. In its reconfigurations of scale and scope and its temporal and spatial translations of universal time and space, *Voyage of Time* articulates its multiple temporalities by way of, and thus inscribing, the representational technologies and screen architectures of the present and past in ongoing dialogue, as these intertwined histories – cosmic and cinematic – continue to unfurl.

The Deep (and High and Wide) Time of Cinema

In addition to representation, in these conceptions of cosmic and cinematic time, what might the deep temporal case study of *Voyage of Time* reveal about the history of cinema more generally (or genealogically)? To abstract, we might further link ideas of cosmic history and cinema history in terms of specific notions of deep time and the media archaeological models that seek to account for it outside of science. The comparative imaging of *Voyage of Time* encourages an expanded frame (or frames), situating the history of IMAX, for example, as just one moment within the history of cinema and situating the history of cinema within the history of the moving image. These ideas are evolutionary, but not necessarily linear – taking cues from science, in terms of the temporal and historiographic frameworks we might utilise in understanding the history of cinema and its temporal spans. Such time is deep, to an extent, but also high and wide, to playfully extend this notion.

Indeed, deep time is often used in the field of media archaeology, including in what Zielinski terms the 'deep time of the media' (Zielinski 2006 [2002]), detailing analogies between the history of the earth and that of sound and image. The principal impulse, in line with the concerns of scientific discourses, is to deepen our historical – and historiographic – models and the metaphors and analogies used therein. In terms of cinema, the shift is away from an account of a medium whose evolutionary history is linear, fixed and determined, towards models that are dynamic, fluid and complex. If film history has often been concerned with an origin story rooted in a discrete moment of birth or invention, for example, media archaeology, by contrast, encourages us to consider alternative temporal structures, viewing history (or histories) over much greater periods of time and via alternative or parallel genealogies.

For Zielinski, in particular, the emphasis is not on any single medium or technical configuration, but rather an overarching focus on 'hearing and seeing by technical means' (Zielinski 2006 [2002]). This is proposed as an alternative or corrective to more traditional histories, wherein narrowly defined (and thus problematic) teleologies of progress map trajectories of media history that are both singular and inevitable. Zielinski's deep time, by comparison, explicitly eschews a linear, evolutionary model, which he describes as the fallacy of 'the idea of inexorable, quasi-natural, technical progress' (Zielinski 2006 [2002]: 3). By contrast, deep time paints what Zielinski describes as

> a very different picture of what has hitherto been called progress. The notion of continuous progress from lower to higher, from simple to complex, must be abandoned, together with all the images, metaphors, and iconography that have been – and still are – used to describe progress. (Zielinski 2006 [2002]: 5)

Notably, in making this argument, Zielinski identifies IMAX in particular as one such teleological marker, describing and critiquing an evolutionary history that comprises what he terms a 'cinema archaeology (from the cave paintings of Lascaux to the immersive IMAX)' (Zielinski 2006 [2002]: 2). A cinema archaeology drawn along such lines would point simply to a linear progression, a teleology of incremental shifts that eventually arrive at a contemporary moment of full realisation, as retrospectively charted from a post hoc perspective.

In this context, recalling the geology of McPhee's basin and range, it is significant that McPhee's ultimate vision of geological formations is cyclical (McPhee 1981) – a connection noted by Zielinski himself (Zielinski 2006 [2002]: 5) and a view with considerable consequences not only for our understanding of the history of the earth, but for how we approach historiography of any kind, including with regard to cinema. Yet even while referencing the ideas of science, as if to sound a warning as to the potential reductiveness of such notions as pure metaphor, Zielinski also reminds us that '[a]n investigation of the deep time of media attractions must provide more than a simple analogy between the findings of research on the history of earth and its organisms and the evolution of technical media' (Zielinski 2006 [2002]: 7).

If this chapter has adopted, adapted and added to such metaphors in its discussion of *Voyage of Time*, it has also sought to expand on a simple analogy between the history of the cosmos on the one hand, and the history of cinema on the other, in order to suggest how such metaphors might be actively applied to our understandings of film history – that is, how we might utilise cosmological and other scientific concepts as historiographic tools.

Voyage of Time offers a more literal level of subject matter – its own vision of evolutionary history – in addition to the historiography implicit in its deep temporal representations. It foregrounds the cyclical nature of life on the planet, while simultaneously presenting an overarching movement from past to present to future in its deep temporal framing, from the origins of the known universe to its ultimate finitude and the question of thereafter.

Plotted in linear, evolutionary terms, the teleological history that Zielinski critiques – specifically, from Lascaux to IMAX – would point, in more recent times, to a succession of developments that ostensibly advance the origins of what we might call the cinematic species, in terms of its own particular technical media, in Zielinski's words. That is: approximately fifty years ago, in 1970, the first IMAX film, *Tiger Child* (Donald Brittain), was premiered at Expo '70 in Osaka, Japan; one year later, the world's first permanent IMAX installation was launched at the Cinesphere theatre in Toronto, Canada; IMAX theatres proliferated in the next decades until the present of *Voyage of Time: The IMAX Experience* (including its 3.6:1 Ultra Widescreen presentation) and continue into the future.

From a less teleologically fixed perspective, however, we might also move backwards and forwards in time, and do so more fluidly via the multiple continuities that connect the pre-cinematic to the post-cinematic in terms of deep time and the impulses and endeavours that mirror practices and approaches across history. We might move from side to side, too, as deep time is elastically imagined as a high time and a wide time. Such notions are especially apt in the context of the more literally expanded frames, ratios and screens of *Voyage of Time* and an expanded historical purview that seeks to connect imaging across otherwise discrete fields. If this is an evolutionary history of the moving image modelled on science, it is one of diversification as well as convergence, revealing dynamic flows of cinematic time and the proliferation and interaction of overlapping histories.

Indeed, one of the aims of media archaeology is to chart film history in contexts other than the traditionally cinematic. For Thomas Elsaesser, for example, it is to open up to other fields. An understanding of film history cognisant of deeper temporality, he argues,

> does not insist on cinema's uniqueness as an art form and its specificity as a medium. Instead, it sees cinema's past as well as its future firmly embedded in other media practices, other technologies, other social uses, and above all as having – throughout its history – interacted with, been dependent on, been complemented by, and found itself in competition with all manner of entertainment forms, scientific pursuits, practical applications, military uses. (Elsaesser 2016: 19)

The focus is on a plurality of contexts, applications and histories, interconnecting branches that each have distinct lineage, but which are nevertheless part of the same species, genus or family.

In the instance of *Voyage of Time*, as Elsaesser might suggest, science and cinema are likewise interwoven. One could see in Malick's treatment of cosmic time, for example, the depth of cinematic time, recalling an archaeology of cinema (in the film's cyclical connections with the histories of IMAX, widescreen cinema, expanded cinema and so on) but also one of science, expanding our definition of the cinematic in the intersections of the tools and practices of visualisation (from the microscope to visual effects) and exhibition (from the planetarium to IMAX).

If *Voyage of Time* explicitly grapples with the evolutionary scales and models of science, it implicitly grapples with those of cinema, too, in terms of how we might historicise the moving image. Across the film's multiple technologies spanning parallel fields, we witness evolution as a series of intersecting apparatuses, connecting imaging in ostensibly discrete realms – expressly cinematic in part, but also, in its historical and other continuities, simply hearing and seeing by technical means, in Zielinski's terms. Ultimately, whether deep, high or wide, *Voyage of Time* suggests an expanded temporal frame for how we might think about the moving image, across fields and across time.

CONCLUSION

'Historians of science are very good at demonstrating the dialectical relationship between tools, theories, and representations', argues Curtis (2013: 46). After all, he explains, 'any given technology is not a single thing, but multiply adaptable to various agendas' (Curtis 2013: 47). Historians of film, we might add, must likewise consider the multiple uses of any given technology. These include the particular interstices of the various agendas bound up in *Voyage of Time*, for example, and its own tools, theories and representations, a range of imaging devices and the images they produce, spanning both science and cinema. In Malick's film, these tools of visualisation, theories of deep time and representations of the universe collectively constitute one such dialectical relationship.

To extrapolate, in media archaeological terms, *Voyage of Time* evidences a genealogical branching of the moving image and the continuities of deep time. This trajectory includes the cinematic, in terms of a specific conception of the medium and its history, but is also more fluid, multiply adaptable to various agendas, as Curtis suggests. In terms of evolutionary history, this eschews linear notions of Darwinian survival of the fittest in favour of the configurational continuities and flows of dynamic ecosystems – preceding, succeeding and in parallel realms to the cinematic. To Zielinski and others, the deep time of science can also be applied to the history of the moving image: while it is certainly not the macro span of many billions of years as depicted in *Voyage of Time*, it is nevertheless deeper than one might imagine, transcending the thin descriptions and causal narrative arcs of quotidian historical discourses.

On such macro scales, literal and figurative frames span both the expanses of the cosmos and the evolving histories of scientific visualisation and cinematic representation, encompassing the respective disciplines and practices

and also the multiple intersections that exist in laboratories and movie theatres. The suggestion is not a finite or discrete evolutionary linearity, rather
a series of overlapping concerns as articulated via an expanding universe – in
metaphorical terms – of technologies, screens and images, with the historical
dialogue between science and cinema just one example.

In connecting cosmological and cinematic histories via scientific and cinematic apparatuses, Malick's own history of time might thus be read in microcosm as the story of cinematic time in terms of the evolution of the medium
and an expanded history (or histories) of the moving image. In this particular
reading, *Voyage of Time* also becomes the larger journey of the cinematic –
cosmic luminescence across screens, across media and as temporally and
spatially experienced.

Notes

CHAPTER I

1. This montage excerpts *The Butler and the Maid* (Anon., 1912), *The Mysterious Mrs. M* (Lois Weber, 1917), *Draga, the Gypsy* (Otis Turner, 1913), *The Unpardonable Sin* (Barry O'Neil, 1916), *The Little Orphan* (Jack Conway, 1917), *A Christmas Accident* (Harold M. Shaw, 1912), *Polly of the Circus* (Charles T. Horan and Edwin L. Hollywood, 1917), *Her Soul's Inspiration* (Jack Conway, 1916), *The Iron Hand* (Ulysses Davis, 1916), *Daybreak* (Anon., 1913), *What Is the Use of Repining?* (Dell Henderson, 1913), *The Martyrs* (Anon., 1912) and *The Social Buccaneer* (Jack Conway, 1916).
2. See, for example, *Decasia* (2002), a collage film of images compiled from early cinema, in which the decay of nitrate film and the metaphorical properties associated with it become central subject matter.
3. While it is beyond the scope of this particular study, the relationship in *Dawson City: Frozen Time* between the damaged film image and its depiction of the physical devastation of the natural environment offers a productive entry point into wider debates around the environmental impact of cinema and its own mined materials; see, for example, Vaughan (2019).
4. Morrison details a proprietary process that uses the Isadora real-time audio–visual effects software to program what he terms 'noise design' as well as 'sound design' (Crafton with Morrison 2018: 99).
5. In an irony that says much about the status of this medium in the contemporary moment, it is worth noting that this film about film is distributed only as a digital print.

CHAPTER 2

1. For more general histories of the drone in military, surveillance and other applications, see, for example, Chamayou (2015 [2013]), Gusterson (2016).
2. Similarly, one could point to Virilio's proclamation – in his paraphrasing of artist Nam June Paik – that 'Cinema Isn't I See, It's I Fly' (Virilio 1989 [1984]: 11–30), a notion that has never been truer in the instance of the camera-carrying drone.

CHAPTER 3

1. See, for example, data compiled by the Motion Picture Association of America (MPAA) and its 'Theatrical and Home Entertainment Market Environment' report for calendar year 2017, according to which consumer spending on theatrical cinema has long since been surpassed by the non-theatrical alternatives of what the report terms 'physical home entertainment' and 'digital home entertainment', with theatrical expenditure accounting for 35 per cent of combined '2017 U.S. theatrical and home entertainment consumer spending' (MPAA 2018: 31), and thus already a minority means of experiencing a film in the United States, as one example.

2. Numerous critics, historians and theorists have addressed the existential-historiographic metaphor of cinema's life cycle (in simple terms, a moment of birth followed by a moment of death), responding to the technological and cultural shifts of recent decades, most often with regard to the decline in attendance of movie theatres and the obsolescence of the materiality of physical film, the marginalisation of a culture of cinephilia and the general erosion of the status of cinema as a mass medium.

3. Rodowick's question is itself a past-tense, post-death reframing of André Bazin's famously uttered 'What is cinema?' (Qu'est-ce que le cinéma?), in a series of volumes published between 1958 and 1962, selections of which were later translated into English. See André Bazin (1967/1971).

4. Beyond Kiarostami's features, the short film *Where Is My Romeo?* illustrates the same production process and aesthetic. Specifically, it compiles footage that is similar or even identical to that of *Shirin*, here accompanied by the soundtrack of an actual film, *Romeo and Juliet* (Franco Zeffirelli, 1968), whose titular lovers are broadly akin to Khosrow and Shirin in Persian literary lore and share the amplified affective register associated with romantic tragedy. In terms of a broader culture of historically specific cinephilia and its relation to the movie theatre, *Where Is My Romeo?* forms part of *To Each His Own Cinema* (*Chacun son cinéma: une déclaration d'amour au grand écran*, multiple directors, 2007), an anthology film commissioned for the sixtieth anniversary of the Festival de Cannes. The subtitle of the film reads in translation, 'A declaration of love to the big screen'.

5. For a more detailed discussion of the gendered construction of this audience, see Sara Saljoughi (2012).

6. In a broader context, this cinematic gaze exists in relation to the looking (and being looked at) of a social gaze and the social dimension of spectatorship, particularly when this gaze is gendered. Placed within historical and national contexts (in this instance, the post-revolutionary Iranian state of the Islamic Republic of Iran), alongside a film-theoretical context (the gaze), the gendering of *Shirin*'s represented spectators is a significant representational strategy. For discussion of the film in the context of post-revolutionary visuality and relationships between public and private spaces, which structure acts of looking at faces that would otherwise most likely be veiled, see Saljoughi (2012). For Saljoughi, in situating this act of looking within the particular politics of Iran and its cinema, 'Kiarostami is certainly making a statement, however elusive and slippery, about the status of women in the cinema and in Iran' (Saljoughi 2012: 526), including in the film's 'fixation with the concept of the gaze as both constitutive and reflective of the spectator's subjectivity' (Saljoughi 2012: 520). Elsewhere, for discussion of the so-called modesty laws introduced by the Ministry of Culture and Islamic Guidance, and which include specific rules concerning women wearing the hijab on screen, see Negar Mottahedeh (2008).

7. Ironically, in what would be a temporal fold of memory, affect and reflexivity, one of the cinematic ghosts this remembrance *might* have conjured is a real cinematic retelling of the story of Shirin, as opposed to Kiarostami's retrospective, audio-only rendering. At least one such Iranian film exists: *Shirin and Farhad* (*Shirin va Farhad*, Abdolhossein Sepanta, 1934).

8. Comprising *Dr. Mabuse, the Gambler* (*Dr. Mabuse, der Spieler*, 1922), *The Testament of Dr. Mabuse* (*Das Testament des Dr. Mabuse*, 1933) and *The 1000 Eyes of Dr. Mabuse* (*Die 1000 Augen des Dr. Mabuse*, 1960).

9. As a brief aside: The Wapping Project closed its doors at this venue in 2013, a reminder of the transience of any cultural geography, which Sinclair also foregrounds in the retrospective transcription of his documented introduction to this site-specific screening, now framed as an interrupted and prematurely terminated act: 'Recording discontinued. No battery life. The Wapping Project [. . .] closed its doors for good in December 2013' (Sinclair 2014: 63).

10. The Odeon Dalston (close to Dalston Junction in the London borough of Hackney), filmed by Smith in 1976, no longer exists. This movie theatre opened in 1939 and closed in 1979, three years after Smith's film, and stood empty until 1984 when it was demolished and later replaced by an apartment block. See Cinema Treasures (2005).

11. As just one example of an illuminating parallel account of a city and its movie theatres as they exist in the contemporary moment and thus in a dynamic between working theatres and historical sites, see *Cinemas of Paris* (Frodon and Iordanova 2016).

CHAPTER 4

1. Originally published in French as 'Le cinéma est-il mortel?', *L'Observateur politique, économique et littéraire*, 13 August 1953, pp. 23–4.

2. According to its closing credits, the film was '[i]nspired by the book *A Man Who Can Recall Past Lives* by Phra Sripariyattiweti, Sang Arun Forest Monastery, Khon Kaen. Published 23 August 1983'.

3. See also *The Primitive Project* (2009), a collection of installations and short films, including *A Letter to Uncle Boonmee* (2009), to which *Uncle Boonmee Who Can Recall His Past Lives* might be considered an extension. These works explore the north-east of Thailand in terms of its legacy of violence and the continued resonance of historical and political memory.

4. In this respect, *Uncle Boonmee Who Can Recall His Past Lives* is a continuation of Apichatpong's recurring authorial concern with film history, filmic obsolescence and the possible afterlives of cinema, explored most explicitly in *The Adventure of Iron Pussy* (*Hua jai tor ra nong*, 2003, co-directed with Michael Shaowanasai), which recreates the otherwise archaic film-based production practices and aesthetics of the Thai film studios of the past.

5. As described in Plato's *The Republic*, *c.*360 BCE.

CHAPTER 5

1. All translations from the original French are mine, unless otherwise noted.

2. *Adieu au langage* is typically translated into English as *Goodbye to Language* or *Farewell to Language*, though neither translation quite captures the specificity of linguistic meanings associated with the word *adieu* and which are addressed in detail elsewhere in this chapter in the specific context of Godard's exploration of language, cinematic and other.

3. While *Goodbye to Language* also exists in a 2D version, it should principally be thought of as a 3D film, and it is this version – or spectatorial experience – that is analysed in this chapter.

4. For extended discussion of Godard's distinctive apparatus, see Corfield (2014), Dallas (2014), Ross (2016), Utterson (2017).

5. For reference, *Goodbye to Language* premiered at the Festival de Cannes on 21 May 2014 and *The Three Disasters* at the same venue on 23 May 2013.

6. Reflexively revealing its apparatus, the closing credits of *Goodbye to Language* even list the various manufacturers, devices and frame rates – 'Canon 23.98, Fuji 24, Mini Sony 29.97, Flip Flop 30, Go Pro 15, Lumix 25' – used in the film's production – and, by all appearances, that of *The Three Disasters*, too – documenting the exact sources of the heterogeneous mixture of devices and formats whose sounds and images the spectator will have just experienced.

7. A text that includes a eulogy that Derrida delivered at Levinas's funeral, thus directly addressing the word *adieu* in the context of mortal passing.

CHAPTER 6

1. *Voyage of Time* exists in a number of different versions, distributed under a number of different titles, though its on-screen title card – simply, 'Voyage of Time' – remains the same in all instances. Principally, *Voyage of Time* exists in an approximately forty-five-minute version intended for IMAX exhibition, distributed under the title *Voyage of Time: The IMAX Experience*. This can be viewed alongside a feature-length version intended for non-IMAX exhibition, distributed under the title *Voyage of Time: Life's Journey*. Notably, in addition to the specifics of exhibition, each of these versions is differentiated on the level of content, including alternative voiceover narrations and narrators (Brad Pitt and Cate Blanchett, respectively). Last, a further version is distributed under the title *Voyage of Time: The IMAX Experience in Ultra Widescreen 3.6*, which is essentially *The IMAX Experience* projected in altered aspect ratio in a limited release.

2. More precisely, an estimated 13.799 ± 0.021 billion years, as calculated in 2015 using data derived from the European Space Agency (ESA) Planck space observatory. See Planck Collaboration XIII (2016).

3. For their scholarship in suggesting a range of productive intersections of scientific and cinematic temporalities, I am indebted to Hannah Goodwin and Stephan Boman and their 'Visualizing Deep Time' panel, convened at the Society for Cinema and Media Studies (SCMS) 57th Annual Conference, Chicago, Illinois, 24 March 2017, at which elements of this chapter were presented.

4. A visualisation produced by Andrew Hamilton at JILA, a partnership of the University of Colorado Boulder and National Institute of Standards and Technology (NIST).

5. A visualisation produced by James Geach of the Centre for Astrophysics Research (CAR) at the University of Hertfordshire and Robert Crain of the Astrophysics Research Institute (ARI) at Liverpool John Moores University.

6. A visualisation produced by Philip Hopkins and Christopher Hayward, Theoretical AstroPhysics Including Relativity and Cosmology (TAPIR) at the California Institute of Technology.

7. The Milky Way is predicted to collide with its neighbouring Andromeda Galaxy (aka Messier 31 or NGC 224) in approximately four billion years.

8. For underlying imagery sourced from the NASA Hubble Space Telescope, see www.spacetelescope.org/images/heic0604a.

9. For the archive gallery of the NASA Solar Dynamics Laboratory, see sdo.gsfc.nasa.gov.

10. For underlying imagery sourced from the European Southern Observatory (ESO) MPG/ESO 2.2-metre telescope in La Silla, Chile, see www.eso.org/public/archives/images/original/eso1105a.tif.

11. Exhibition data according to the Motion Picture Association of America (MPAA) 2016 'Theatrical Market Statistics' report (MPAA 2017: 21).

12. A visualisation produced by Tom Abel and Ralf Kähler at the Kavli Institute for Particle Astrophysics and Cosmology (KIPAC), a joint laboratory of Stanford University and the SLAC National Accelerator Laboratory.

Bibliography

Aaron, Michele (2014), *Death and the Moving Image: Ideology, Iconography and I*, Edinburgh: Edinburgh University Press.

Balsom, Erika (2015), 'Parallax Plurality', *Artforum*, 54.1: 354–61, 408.

Barber, Stephen (2010), *Abandoned Images: Film and Film's End*, London: Reaktion Books.

Barthes, Roland (1986 [1975]), 'Leaving the Movie Theater', in *The Rustle of Language*, trans. Richard Howard, New York: Farrar, Straus and Giroux, pp. 345–9.

Batcho, James (2018), *Terrence Malick's Unseeing Cinema: Memory, Time and Audibility*, Cham, Switzerland: Palgrave Macmillan.

Baudry, Jean-Louis (1976 [1975]), 'The Apparatus', trans. Jean Andrews and Bertrand Augst, *Camera Obscura*, 1.1: 104–26.

Bazin, André (1960 [1945]), 'The Ontology of the Photographic Image', trans. Hugh Gray, *Film Quarterly*, 13.4: 4–9.

Bazin, André (1967/1971), *What Is Cinema?*, Vols. 1 and 2, trans. Hugh Gray, Berkeley, CA: University of California Press.

Bazin, André (2014 [1953]), 'Is Cinema Mortal?', in Dudley Andrew (ed.), *André Bazin's New Media*, trans. Dudley Andrew, Oakland, CA: University of California Press, pp. 313–17.

Bellour, Raymond (1992), '[Not] Just an Other Filmmaker', in Raymond Bellour and Mary Lea Bandy (eds), *Jean-Luc Godard: Son + Image, 1974–1991*, trans. Lynne Kirby, New York: The Museum of Modern Art, pp. 215–31.

Bellour, Raymond (2007), 'For Ever Divided', in Michael Temple, James S. Williams and Michael Witt (eds), *For Ever Godard*, trans. Michael Temple, James S. Williams and Michael Witt, London: Black Dog Publishing, pp. 11–13.

Benson-Allott, Caetlin (2013), *Killer Tapes and Shattered Screens: Video Spectatorship from VHS to File Sharing*, Berkeley, CA: University of California Press.

Bergala, Alain (2016 [2006]), *The Cinema Hypothesis: Teaching Cinema in the Classroom and Beyond*, trans. Madeline Whittle, Vienna: FilmmuseumSynemaPublikationen.

Bordwell, David (2014), 'Say Hello to *Goodbye to Language*', *David Bordwell's Website on Cinema*, 2 November 2014, <http://www.davidbordwell.net/blog/2014/11/02/say-hello-to-goodby-to-language>.

Bozovic, Marijeta (2016), 'The Ark Sinks: Alexander Sokurov's *Francofonia*', *Los Angeles Review of Books*, 8 July 2016, <http://lareviewofbooks.org/article/ark-sinks-alexander-sokurovs-francofonia>.

Cameron, Allan (2012), 'Zombie Media: Transmission, Reproduction, and the Digital Dead', *Cinema Journal*, 52.1: 66–89.

Casetti, Francesco (2015), *The Lumière Galaxy: Seven Key Words for the Cinema to Come*, New York: Columbia University Press.

Cavell, Stanley (1971), *The World Viewed: Reflections on the Ontology of Film*, New York: The Viking Press.

Chamayou, Grégoire (2015 [2013]), *A Theory of the Drone*, trans. Janet Lloyd, New York: The New Press.

Cherchi Usai, Paolo (2001), *The Death of Cinema: History, Cultural Memory and the Digital Dark Age*, London: BFI.

Cherchi Usai, Paolo (2011), 'Paolo Cherchi Usai', in Nicholas Cullinan (ed.), *Tacita Dean: Film*, London: Tate Publishing, p. 60.

Chion, Michel (1994 [1990]), *Audio-Vision: Sound on Screen*, trans. Claudia Gorbman, New York: Columbia University Press.

Chion, Michel (1999 [1982]), *The Voice in Cinema*, trans. Claudia Gorbman, New York: Columbia University Press.

Christiansen, Steen Ledet (2017), *Drone Age Cinema: Action Film and Sensory Assault*, London: I. B. Tauris.

Cinema Treasures (2005), 'Odeon Dalston', *Cinema Treasures*, 22 December 2005, <cinematreasures.org/theaters/14818>.

Conley, Tom (2007), *Cartographic Cinema*, Minneapolis, MN: University of Minnesota Press.

Corfield, David (2014), 'In Conversation with Jean-Luc Godard: Filmmaker Extraordinaire', *Canon Europe*, 21 May 2014, <http://cpn.canon-europe.com/content/Jean-Luc_Godard.do>.

Crafton, Donald, with Bill Morrison (2018), 'A Deal with the Devil: Bill Morrison on *Dawson City: Frozen Time*', *The Moving Image*, 18.1: 92–103.

Curtis, Scott (2013), 'Science Lessons', *Film History*, 25.1–2: 45–54.

Dagen, Philippe and Franck Nouchi (2014), 'Jean-Luc Godard: "Le cinéma, c'est un oubli de la réalité"', *Le Monde*, 12 June 2014, pp. 18–19.

Dallas, Paul (2014), '1 + 1 = 3', *Film Comment*, 50.6: 38–9.

Daney, Serge (2007 [1986]), 'For Ever Divided', in Michael Temple, James S. Williams and Michael Witt (eds), *For Ever Godard*, trans. Michael Temple, James S. Williams and Michael Witt, London: Black Dog Publishing, pp. 68–71.

Debord, Guy-Ernest (1957), *Guide psychogéographique de Paris: Discours sur les passions de l'amour*, Copenhagen: Permild & Rosengreen.

Debord, Guy-Ernest (1981 [1955]), 'Introduction to a Critique of Urban Geography', in Ken Knabb (ed.), *Situationist International Anthology*, trans. Ken Knabb, Berkeley, CA: Bureau of Public Secrets, pp. 5–8.

Derrida, Jacques (1994 [1993]), *Specters of Marx: The State of the Debt, the Work of Mourning & the New International*, trans. Peggy Kamuf, London: Routledge.

Derrida, Jacques (1995 [1992]), *The Gift of Death*, trans. David Wills, Chicago, IL: University of Chicago Press.

Derrida, Jacques (1999 [1997]), *Adieu to Emmanuel Levinas*, trans. Pascale-Anne Brault and Michael Naas, Stanford, CA: Stanford University Press.

Doane, Mary Ann (2002), *The Emergence of Cinematic Time: Modernity, Contingency, the Archive*, Cambridge, MA: Harvard University Press.

Elsaesser, Thomas (2005), 'Cinephilia or the Uses of Disenchantment', in Marijke de Valck and Malte Hagener (eds), *Cinephilia: Movies, Love and Memory*, Amsterdam: Amsterdam University Press, pp. 27–43.

Elsaesser, Thomas (2012), 'Is Nothing New? Turn-of-the-Century Epistemes in Film History', in André Gaudreault, Nicolas Dulac and Santiago Hidalgo (eds), *A Companion to Early Cinema*, Chichester: John Wiley & Sons, pp. 587–609.

Elsaesser, Thomas (2016), *Film History as Media Archaeology: Tracking Digital Cinema*, Amsterdam: Amsterdam University Press.

Fife Donaldson, Lucy (2014), *Texture in Film*, London: Palgrave Macmillan.

Fisher, Mark (2012), 'What Is Hauntology?', *Film Quarterly*, 66.1: 16–24.

Fisher, Mark (2014), *Ghosts of My Life: Writings on Depression, Hauntology and Lost Futures*, London: Zero Books.

Fowler, Catherine (2012), 'Remembering Cinema "Elsewhere": From Retrospection to Introspection in the Gallery Film', *Cinema Journal*, 51.2: 26–45.

Fox, Albertine (2018), *Godard and Sound: Acoustic Innovation in the Late Films of Jean-Luc Godard*, London: I. B. Tauris.

Freud, Sigmund (1957 [1917]), 'Mourning and Melancholia', in James Strachey (ed.), *The Standard Edition of the Complete Psychological Works of Sigmund Freud*, Vol. 14, trans. James Strachey, London: The Hogarth Press, pp. 243–58.

Frodon, Jean-Michel and Dina Iordanova (eds) (2016), *Cinemas of Paris*, St Andrews: St Andrews Film Studies.

Fronty, François (2009), 'Shirin of a Hundred Faces', trans. Matthew Cunningham, *Cahiers du Cinéma in English*, February: 82–3.

Gaudreault, André and Philippe Marion (2015 [2013]), *The End of Cinema? A Medium in Crisis in the Digital Age*, trans. Timothy Barnard, New York: Columbia University Press.

Godard, Jean-Luc and Youssef Ishaghpour (2005 [2000]), *Cinema: The Archeology of Film and the Memory of a Century*, trans. John Howe, New York: Berg.

Gray, Carmen (2015), 'War Paint: *Francofonia* Director Alexander Sokurov Talks Art and Power', *The Calvert Journal*, 17 September 2015, <http://www.calvertjournal.com/articles/show/4695/sokurov-interview-Francofonia-venice>.

Green, Ronald (2014), *Buddhism Goes to the Movies: Introduction to Buddhist Thought and Practice*, New York: Routledge.

Griffiths, Alison (2008), *Shivers Down Your Spine: Cinema, Museums, and the Immersive View*, New York: Columbia University Press.

Grønstad, Asbjørn (2012), 'Abbas Kiarostami's Shirin and the Aesthetics of Ethical Intimacy', *Film Criticism*, 37.2: 22–37.

Gusterson, Hugh (2016), *Drone: Remote Control Warfare*, Cambridge, MA: MIT Press.

Hadjioannou, Markos (2012), *From Light to Byte: Toward an Ethics of Digital Cinema*, Minneapolis, MN: University of Minnesota Press.

Hoberman, J. (2012), *Film after Film: Or, What Became of 21st-Century Cinema?*, London: Verso.

Hopwood, Henry V. (1899), *Living Pictures: Their History, Photo-Production and Practical Working*, London: The Optician & Photographic Trades Review.

Ingawanij, May Adadol (2013), 'Animism and the Performative Realist Cinema of Apichatpong Weerasethakul', in Anat Pick and Guinevere Narraway (eds), *Screening Nature: Cinema beyond the Human*, Oxford: Berghahn Books, pp. 91–109.

Jacobowitz, Florence and Richard Lippe (2015), 'The Man with the Movie Camera: Godard's *Adieu au langage*', *CineAction*, 96: 24–5.

Jones, J. R. (2017), 'Digging for Old', *Chicago Reader*, 46.51: 13–18.

Kaplan, Caren (2018), *Aerial Aftermaths: Wartime from Above*, Durham, NC: Duke University Press.

Khodaei, Khatereh (2009), '*Shirin* as Described by Kiarostami', *Offscreen*, 13.1, <http://www.offscreen.com/view/shirin_kiarostami>.

Kittler, Friedrich A. (1999 [1986]), *Gramophone, Film, Typewriter*, trans. Geoffrey Winthrop-Young and Michael Wutz, Stanford, CA: Stanford University Press.

Kroiter, Roman (1970), 'IMAX at Expo '70', *American Cinematographer*, 51.8: 772–3, 798–9.

Kuhn, Annette, Daniel Biltereyst and Philippe Meers (2017), 'Memories of Cinemagoing and Film Experience: An Introduction', *Memory Studies*, 10.1: 3–16.

Kula, Sam (1979), 'There's Film in Them Thar Hills!', *American Film*, 4.9: 14–18.

Levinas, Emmanuel (1986 [1982]), 'Bad Conscience and the Inexorable', in Richard A. Cohen (ed.), *Face to Face with Levinas*, trans. Richard A. Cohen, Albany, NY: State University of New York Press, pp. 35–40.

Lovatt, Philippa (2013), '"Every drop of my blood sings our song. There, can you hear it?": Haptic Sound and Embodied Memory in the Films of Apichatpong Weerasethakul', *The New Soundtrack*, 3.1: 61–79.

Macaulay, Scott (2017), 'Explosive Memories: Five Questions for *Dawson City: Frozen Time* Director Bill Morrison', *Filmmaker*, 9 June 2017, <http://filmmakermagazine.com/tag/dawson-city-frozen-time/#.XRuZB2bMzOQ>.

MacDonald, Scott (2016), 'The Filmmaker as Miner: An Interview with Bill Morrison', *Cineaste*, 42.1: 40–3.

McPhee, John (1981), *Basin and Range*, New York: Farrar, Straus and Giroux.

Morgan, Daniel (2012), *Late Godard and the Possibilities of Cinema*, Berkeley and Los Angeles, CA: University of California Press.

Morrison, Bill (2018), 'Film as Social Memory: Bill Morrison on *Dawson City: Frozen Time*', *Walker Reader*, 2 March 2018, <http://walkerart.org/magazine/film-as-social-memory-bill-morrison-on-dawson-city-frozen-time>.

Motion Picture Association of America (MPAA) (2017), 'Theatrical Market Statistics', *Motion Picture Association of America (MPAA)*, 22 March 2017, <mpaa.org/research-docs/2016-theatrical-market-statistics-report>.

Motion Picture Association of America (MPAA) (2018), 'Theatrical and Home Entertainment Market Environment (THEME) Report', *Motion Picture Association of America (MPAA)*, 4 April 2018, <mpaa.org/wp-content/uploads/2018/04/MPAA-THEME-Report-2017_Final.pdf>.

Mottahedeh, Negar (2008), *Displaced Allegories: Post-Revolutionary Iranian Cinema*, Durham, NC: Duke University Press.

Mulvey, Laura (2006), *Death 24x a Second: Stillness and the Moving Image*, London: Reaktion Books.

Naficy, Hamid (2012), *A Social History of Iranian Cinema, Vol. 4: The Globalizing Era, 1984–2010*, Durham, NC: Duke University Press.

Naremore, James (2010), 'Films of the Year, 2009', *Film Quarterly*, 63.4: 18–32.

Naremore, James (2011), 'Films of the Year, 2010', *Film Quarterly*, 64.4: 34–47.

Newhall, Beaumont (1969), *Airborne Camera: The World from the Air and Outer Space*, New York: Hastings House.

O'Hara, Angela (2012), 'Mysterious Object of Desire: The Haunted Cinema of Apichatpong Weerasethakul', in Philippa Gates and Lisa Funnell (eds), *Transnational Asian Identities in Pan-Pacific Cinemas: The Reel Asian Exchange*, Abingdon: Routledge, pp. 177–90.

Parikka, Jussi (2015), *A Geology of Media*, Minneapolis, MN: University of Minnesota Press.

Peranson, Mark and Kong Rithdee (2010), 'Ghost in the Machine: Apichatpong Weerasethakul's Letter to Cinema', *Cinema Scope*, 43: 42–7.

Planck Collaboration XIII (2016), 'Planck 2015 Results XIII. Cosmological Parameters', *Astronomy & Astrophysics*, 594.A13: 1–63.

Prince, Stephen (2012), *Digital Visual Effects in Cinema: The Seduction of Reality*, New Brunswick, NJ: Rutgers University Press.

Quandt, James (2011), 'Living Memory', *Artforum*, 49.7: 59–60.

Quandt, James (2014), 'Last Harrumph', *Artforum*, 53.1: 127–8.

Richards, Rashna Wadia (2013), *Cinematic Flashes: Cinephilia and Classical Hollywood*, Bloomington, IN: Indiana University Press.

Rithdee, Kong (2009), 'Cinema of Reincarnations', in James Quandt (ed.), *Apichatpong Weerasethakul*, Vienna: Austrian Film Museum, pp. 118–24.

Rodowick, D. N. (2007), *The Virtual Life of Film*, Cambridge, MA: Harvard University Press.

Roeper, Richard (2016), '*Francofonia*: Love Poem to the Louvre a Work of Art Itself', *Chicago Sun-Times*, 5 May 2016, <http://chicago.suntimes.com/entertainment/francofonia-love-poem-to-the-louvre-a-work-of-art-itself>.

Rogers, Ariel (2013), *Cinematic Appeals: The Experience of New Movie Technologies*, New York: Columbia University Press.

Ross, Miriam (2016), 'Godard's Stereoscopic Illusions: Against a Total Cinema', *Screening the Past*, 41, 21 December 2016, <http://www.screeningthepast.com/2016/12/godards-stereoscopic-illusions-against-a-total-cinema>.

Saljoughi, Sara (2012), 'Seeing Iranian Style: Women and Collective Vision in Abbas Kiarostami's *Shirin*', *Iranian Studies*, 45.4: 519–35.

Scott, A. O. (2014), 'Lots of Philosophy, No Inhibitions', *New York Times*, 29 October 2014, Section C: pp. 1, 5.

Scott, A. O. (2016), 'The Cosmology of Terrence Malick (The Short Version)', *New York Times*, 7 October 2016, Section C: pp. 9.

Sinclair, Iain (2014), *70x70: Unlicensed Preaching – A Life Unpacked in 70 Films*, London: King Mob/Volcano Publishing.

Sontag, Susan (1996), 'The Decay of Cinema', *New York Times Magazine*, 25 February 1996, pp. 60–1.

Stanley, Col. Roy M., II (1981), *World War II Photo Intelligence*, New York: Charles Scribner's Sons.

Taubin, Amy (2014), 'Cannes', *Film Comment*, 50.4: 48–51.

Teh, David (2011), 'Itinerant Cinema: The Social Surrealism of Apichatpong Weerasethakul', *Third Text*, 25.5: 595–609.

Teo, Stephen (2013), *The Asian Cinema Experience: Styles, Spaces, Theory*, Abingdon: Routledge.

Thompson, Kristin and David Bordwell (2014), '*Adieu au langage*: 2 + 2 × 3D', *David Bordwell's Website on Cinema*, 7 September 2014, <http://www.davidbordwell.net/blog/2014/09/07/adieu-au-langage-2-2-x-3d>.

Torlasco, Domietta (2013), *The Heretical Archive: Digital Memory at the End of Film*, Minneapolis, MN: University of Minnesota Press.

Utterson, Andrew (2017), 'Practice Makes Imperfect: The Creative Imperfections of Jean-Luc Godard's Three-Dimensional (3D) Cinema', *Quarterly Review of Film and Video*, 34.3: 295–308.

van Dijck, José (2007), *Mediated Memories in the Digital Age*, Stanford, CA: Stanford University Press.

Vaughan, Hunter (2019), *Hollywood's Dirtiest Secret: The Hidden Environmental Costs of the Movies*, New York: Columbia University Press.

Virilio, Paul (1989 [1984]), *War and Cinema: The Logistics of Perception*, trans. Patrick Camiller, London: Verso.

Voyage of Time official production notes, <voyageoftime.imax.com/#press>.

Voyage of Time official trailer, <voyageoftime.imax.com/#videos>.

Wayman, Erin (2016), '*Voyage of Time* More Art Film Than Documentary', *Science News*, 190.9: 29.

Weerasethakul, Apichatpong (2009 [2007]), 'Ghosts in the Darkness', in James Quandt (ed.), *Apichatpong Weerasethakul*, trans. Vera Pansanga, Vienna: Austrian Film Museum, pp. 104–17.

Weerasethakul, Apichatpong (2010), *Uncle Boonmee Who Can Recall His Past Lives* official press materials, 'Interview with Apichatpong Weerasethakul', unpaginated.

Weerasethakul, Apichatpong (2011), 'November 6, 2552', in Maeve Butler and Eimear O'Raw (eds), *For Tomorrow for Tonight: Apichatpong Weerasethakul*, Dublin: Irish Museum of Modern Art, unpaginated.

Wiseman, Andreas (2015), 'Finding *Francofonia*', *Screen Daily*, 5 September 2015, <http://www.screendaily.com/features-archive/finding-francofonia/5092583.article>.

Witt, Michael (1999), 'The Death(s) of Cinema According to Godard', *Screen*, 40.3: 331–46.

Witt, Michael (2013), *Jean-Luc Godard, Cinema Historian*, Bloomington, IN: Indiana University Press.

Youngblood, Gene (1970), *Expanded Cinema*, New York: Dutton.

Zielinski, Siegfried (2006 [2002]), *Deep Time of the Media: Toward an Archaeology of Hearing and Seeing by Technical Means*, trans. Gloria Custance, Cambridge, MA: MIT Press.

Zimmer, Catherine (2015), *Surveillance Cinema*, New York: New York University Press.

Index